BBC

KS3

Bitesize Revision

BITESIZE revision

Science

Steven Goldsmith

Published by BBC Worldwide Ltd

Woodlands, 80 Wood Lane, London W12 0TT

First published 2003
Reprinted 2005

© Steven Goldsmith/BBC Worldwide Limited 2003.

All rights reserved

ISBN: 0 563 54715 4

The author and Publisher would like to thank QCA for granting permission to use their work.

Illustrations © Oxford Illustrators & Designers Ltd and © Hardlines Ltd.

Printed and bound by Sterling Press Ltd. UK.

BBC

Contents

Photo acknowledgements

Alamy Images p30 (forest/Robert Harding Picture Library Ltd.), p89 (tidal power station/Photofusion Picture Library); Corbis p6 (elephant/Martin Harvey; Gallo Images), p18 (smoker/Tom and Dee Ann McCarthy), p20 (chloroplasts/Lester V. Bergman), p30 (pond Archivo Iconografico, S.A.), p34 (bricks/Nathan Benn; balloons/Alan Schein Photography), p60 (tablet/H. Prinz), p62 (Roger Ressmayer), p81 (Michael Pole), p86 (satellite/T. Kevin Smyth), p89 (solar panels/Chinch Gryniewicz; Ecoscene); Flowerphotos/Mike Bentley p20 (flowers); Getty Images/The Image Bank p24 (dogs/G.K. and Vikki Hart), p34 (swimmer/David Madison), p68 (speed boat/Robert Holland; train/Felix Clonzot; snail/Derek P. Redfearn); Getty Images/Photodisc Blue p30 (desert); Getty Images/Stone p60 (acid rain damage/Oliver Strewe), p89 (wind turbines/A and L Sinibaldi); Getty Images/Taxi p6 (desert flower/Thomas Wiewandt), p24 (family/David Lees), p60 (toothpaste/Frank Saragnese) p68 (runner/V.C.L.); Holt Studios/Nigel Cattlin p22, p60 (lime spreading); NASA p86 (Jupiter); Robert Harding Picture Library Ltd. p18 (bacteria; drugs), p24 (children), p30 (sea shore); Science Photo Library/Oscar Burriel p78.

About *Bitesize*

The BBC revision service, KS3 *Bitesize*, is designed to help you achieve success in the KS3 National Tests.

It includes books, television programmes and a website at **www.bbc.co.uk/bitesize**

Each of these works as a separate resource, designed to help you get the best results.

The television programmes are available on video through your school or you can find out transmission times by calling **08700 100 222**.

About this book

This book is your all-in-one revision companion for the KS3 National Tests. It gives you the three things you need for successful revision:

1 every topic clearly organised and clearly explained

2 the most important facts and ideas highlighted for quick checking

3 all the practice you need.

This book contains a complete set of revision information for pupils taking the level 3–6 and the level 5–7 tiers of tests.

The main areas of science (biology, chemistry and physics) are broken down into several topics. Each topic has a double page in the book. The format of each topic is the same, so you can easily find your way around. The features you can find in each topic are described here:

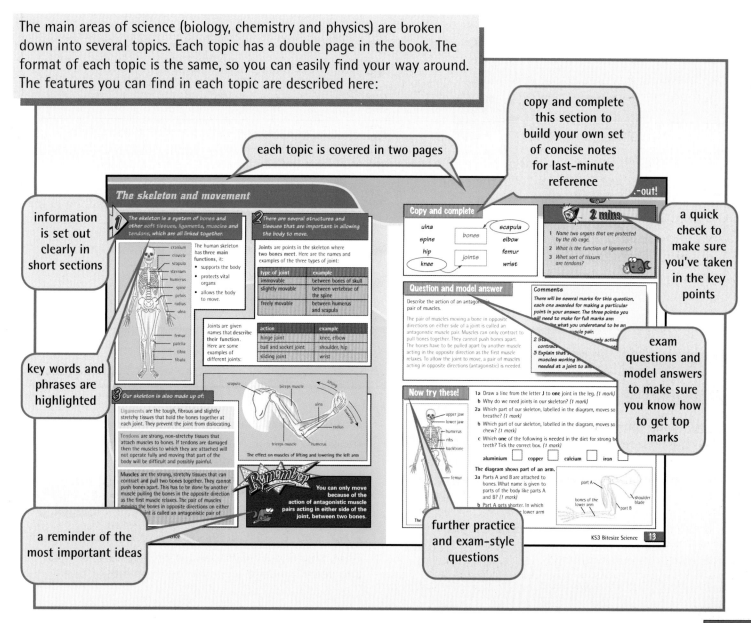

copy and complete this section to build your own set of concise notes for last-minute reference

each topic is covered in two pages

information is set out clearly in short sections

a quick check to make sure you've taken in the key points

key words and phrases are highlighted

exam questions and model answers to make sure you know how to get top marks

a reminder of the most important ideas

further practice and exam-style questions

About the KS3 National Tests

The National Curriculum programme of study for KS3 science is divided into **four attainment targets**:

Sc1	Scientific enquiry
Sc2	Life processes and living things
Sc3	Materials and their properties
Sc4	Physical properties

The National Tests

The Year 9 tests are available in two tiers. The lower tier covers levels 3–6 and the upper tier covers levels 5–7. Your teacher will decide which is best for you and you should know well in advance which tier test you will be taking. There are two papers in each tier, which are both **one hour long**.

Each of the test papers contains questions that cover Sc2, Sc3 and Sc4. From 2003, there will also be a number of questions that test scientific enquiry: Sc1. These questions may be set in unusual contexts, requiring no knowledge of scientific information, asking you to demonstrate an understanding of the processes involved in scientific investigations.

These sorts of questions may ask you to:

- describe how an investigation could be carried out
- identify the factors that need to be controlled
- describe what factors need to be measured
- decide whether the outcome can be predicted
- say how the results are going to be presented
- comment on what the results show and whether they match the prediction
- explain the outcomes
- explain whether the evidence collected is significant, reliable and valid.

Using this book to revise

You'll take your KS3 science tests in early May, so plan your revision carefully. It's a good idea to start your revision two months before this so that you'll have enough time to cover all sections in this book. Don't leave it until the last moment!

Break the subject up into **bite-sized chunks**. That is why this book is divided into small sections. There are 43 topics in this book – how many will you need to cover each week to get it all done in time? You could plan your revision timetable using the contents page. Write the date when you plan to work on each section alongside it.

Don't forget to allow time for revision for your other subjects too.

Make sure you take breaks and have time to relax. Organise your revision around sports, hobbies and your favourite television programmes!

Revising science

If you are actively doing something, you're more likely to remember information.

Write down **important words** and **ideas** as you work through the book. At the end of each section, write down the key facts and ideas from memory.

For a labelled diagram, copy the diagram then close the book and add the labels.

For particular spellings and equations **look**, **cover**, **write** and then **check**.

Write **summary notes** for each section. Rewrite them, copying the originals and then from memory.

Test yourself by writing a key word on one side of a piece of card and the definition or explanation on the other. Revise with a friend, using the cards to test each other.

Record your notes onto a tape and make notes as you listen to yourself reading.

Make a set of revision cards that fit into your pocket – test yourself on your way to school!

Preparing for the tests

The list of equipment you need for the tests doesn't change from year to year: you need a **pen**, **pencil**, **ruler**, **rubber**, **protractor** and **calculator**. If you work in pencil, it's easy to rub out and start again if you get in a mess. If you make a mess of it in pen and have no space left to write another answer, you won't be able to get a fresh copy of the paper to write on and you can't use an extra piece of paper either. Have a sharpener and a couple of ready-sharpened spares handy.

During the test

The markers can only judge how good your answer is by what you write on the paper.

- Read the question carefully before you start to answer, so that you know exactly what is being asked of you.
- Follow all of the instructions in the question.
- When you have to choose a word from a list, use only the words provided.
- Write your answer clearly and precisely.
- If you make a mistake, ensure your first answer is crossed out and that it is clear which answer you want the marker to read.
- Show all your calculations as well as the answer.
- Draw or add to diagrams using a pencil and ruler.
- Do not tick any more boxes than you are asked to in the question.

When you've finished, go back over the paper and:

- attempt any questions or parts you missed out – anything is better than no answer (some people manage to miss out an entire double page)
- work through the questions you've done – you might find a mistake and get some extra marks!

If you have a mobile phone with you, switch it off.

If you don't understand a question, it is worth asking a teacher about it. Remember, the teachers supervising the test have a list of things they are allowed to tell you. If you ask for something that's not on this list they have to refuse to tell you – it's not their fault!

With careful, planned revision you will answer the test questions confidently and gain all the marks you deserve!

Life processes

1 Living things, or *organisms*, are alive because of the processes that go on inside them.

- Each of these **life processes** plays a part in making sure that the organism stays alive.
- Many organisms have organs, which have a special structure to enable them to perform a particular function.

3 Organisms vary in *size* and *complexity*.

- Some organisms are large and **complex** with many different organs. In these organisms several organs are needed for one life process to take place. This group of organs is called an **organ system**.
- Other organisms are simpler with just enough organs to make sure that their life processes take place.

2 The following *seven life processes* are common to all organisms.

Movement: animals can move to find food and safety. Plants move slowly, growing or turning to grow in a particular direction.

Reproduction: all living things are able to produce offspring to replace individuals who die.

Sensitivity: all living things can detect changes both inside and outside them. To survive, they can respond to most of these.

Growth: this is a permanent increase in size that may occur throughout life but particularly when the organism is young.

Respiration: is the release of energy from food for use within the living thing.

Excretion: removes the waste products of chemical reactions which have taken place inside a living thing.

Nutrition: is the process by which living things obtain nutrients. These nutrients provide a source of energy, the raw materials for growth and the substances needed to stay healthy.

4 Here are some examples of the functions of organs in animals and plants, which are involved in these life processes.

function in animals	organ	life process
exerts forces on the skeleton	muscle	movement
collects information from the environment	eye	sensitivity
extracts oxygen from the air	lungs	respiration
removes waste from the blood	kidney	excretion

function in plants	organ	life process
site of photosynthesis	leaf	growth
produces egg cells	ovary	reproduction
absorbs water and dissolved minerals	root hair	nutrition

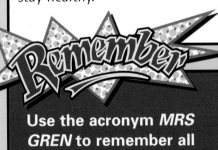

Remember

Use the acronym *MRS GREN* to remember all seven life processes.

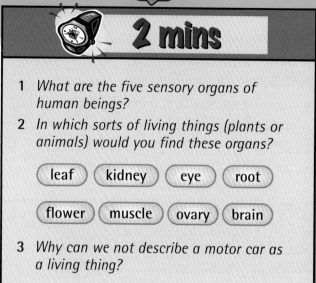

Work-out!

2 mins

1 What are the five sensory organs of human beings?

2 In which sorts of living things (plants or animals) would you find these organs?

(leaf) (kidney) (eye) (root)

(flower) (muscle) (ovary) (brain)

3 Why can we not describe a motor car as a living thing?

Copy and complete

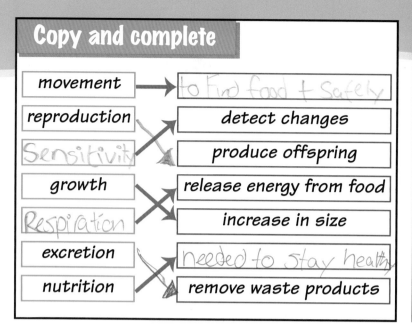

movement	→ to find food + safety
reproduction	detect changes
Sensitivity	produce offspring
growth	release energy from food
Respiration	increase in size
excretion	needed to stay healthy
nutrition	remove waste products

Questions and model answers

1 What is an organ system?

   An organ system is a group of organs that, together, enable a particular life process to take place.

2 Name and give the function of **one** organ in animals that helps the life processes of **a** reproduction and **b** nutrition to take place.

a The ovary produces egg cells, the testes produce sperm cells, the uterus allows the baby to develop inside and the placenta allows matter to pass between mother and baby.

b Teeth crush food in the mouth, the stomach starts digestion of the food and the intestines absorb soluble food.

Comments

The space provided for the answers will give you an idea of how much you need to write to answer a question like this.

The second question may require you to describe the function in detail – so make sure you choose an organ you know well.

Now try these!

The diagram shows a section through a human female reproductive system.

1 a How often are eggs normally released in the female reproductive system? *(1 mark)*

   b In which labelled part is an egg normally fertilised by a sperm? *(1 mark)*

2 Complete the **two** gaps in the sentences below. *(2 marks)*

   A fertilised egg divides into a tiny ball of cells called an embryo. The embryo attaches to the lining of the uterus. Here the embryo grows to become an unborn baby, called a embryo. It takes about 9 months for a baby to develop inside its mother.

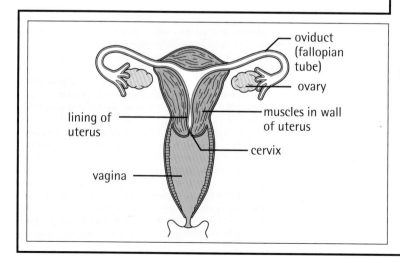

- oviduct (fallopian tube)
- ovary
- muscles in wall of uterus
- cervix
- lining of uterus
- vagina

Cells

1 All organisms are made up of cells.

- Cells are the **smallest units** of all living things. They make up the tissues and organs of all organisms.
- All cells have a **nucleus**, **cytoplasm** and **cell membrane**.

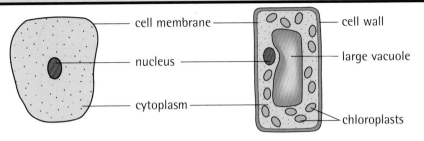

cell membrane — nucleus — cytoplasm

cell wall — large vacuole — chloroplasts

Animal cell   Plant cell

2 The cells of both plants and animals contain three parts.

Cell membrane: this is the outer surface of the cell. It controls what passes into and out of the cell.

Nucleus: this controls the chemical activity of the cell and contains the genetic material.

Cytoplasm: this is the watery, jelly-like liquid that fills the cell. It contains other parts of the cell and is where important chemical reactions take place.

3 Plant cells also have a cell wall, a large vacuole and chloroplasts.

Cell wall: this is outside of the cell membrane. It is made from cellulose and provides support to the cell, helping it to keep its shape.

Large vacuole: this contains a solution of sugars and salts, which is called cell sap. The vacuole is close to the centre of the cell and takes up most of the cell's volume.

Chloroplasts: these contain chlorophyll, a green pigment, which traps light for use in photosynthesis – the process by which plants make their food.

4 There are different sorts of cells in both plants and animals, which have different functions and are adapted in particular ways so they can carry out that function.

  HELP!

These three parts are **not present** in animal cells.

cell	function	structure	
nerve	carries messages around the body		long, thin fibres
red blood	absorbs and carries O_2 around the body		large cell membrane surface area
sperm	fertilises the egg		has a long tail, allowing it move
root hair	absorbs water		large cell membrane surface area
egg	develops into an embryo when fertilised		contains a great deal of cytoplasm
leaf	site of photosynthesis		contains many chloroplasts

Cells may look very different even though they share some common features. This is because each cell has a structure that is adapted to its function.

Copy and complete

Animal cells have:

1 <u>Cell membrane</u>

2 <u>Cytoplasam</u>

3 <u>nucleus</u>

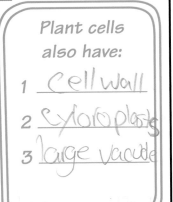

Plant cells also have:

1 <u>Cell wall</u>

2 <u>Cyloroplasts</u>

3 <u>large vacule</u>

2 mins

1 What is the function of the cell membrane?

2 Where, inside a cell, do chemical reactions take place?

3 What is the name of the green-coloured pigment inside chloroplasts?

4 What is the purpose of the cell wall in plant cells?

Questions and model answers

1 How are the structures of the following cells adapted to carry out their particular function?

a **Nerve cell**

Nerve cells have a long, thin, fibrous structure.

b **Root hair cells**

Root hair cells have a cell membrane with a large surface area.

c **Leaf cells**

Leaf cells contain many chloroplasts.

2 What are the functions of the following cells?

a **Red blood cell**

Red blood cells absorb and carry oxygen around the body.

b **Egg cell**

When fertilised, egg cells develop into an embryo.

Comments

The different shapes of the cells enable the different functions. Being able to describe simple cell structure and identify differences between animal and plant cells is required at level 6.

In questions like this, it is important to describe that particular part of the cell which allows it to carry out its particular function and not any other part of the cell. Often this is its shape or the location of particular cell parts.

Now try these!

This cell is from the leaf of a blackberry plant. Four parts of the cell are listed in the table (left).

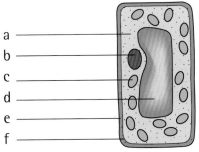

1 Match each name in the table to the correct letter on the diagram. *(4 marks)*

2 Name **two** labelled parts also present in animal cells. Give the correct letters from the diagram. *(2 marks)* b,f

part	letter of part
cell wall	e
cytoplasm	c
nucleus	b
vacuole	d

Food and digestion

1 A *balanced diet* is essential for good health in humans. The components are *carbohydrates, fats, fibre, minerals, proteins, vitamins* **and** *water*.

Few foods contain all of these components, which is why it is important for us all to eat a **variety of foods**, for the following uses:

component	used in the body to	food source
carbohydrates	provide energy	bread, potatoes
fats	store energy	butter, oil
fibre	help the passage of food through the body	vegetables, wholemeal bread
minerals	make and maintain specialist cells	spinach, milk, salt
proteins	grow and to repair the body	meat, fish, cheese
vitamins	control chemical processes	dairy products, fruit, vegetables
water	dissolve food so that it can move through the body	fruit juice, milk, vegetables

2 Not everybody needs the same diet.

- We need different amounts of each component in our diet, depending on our age, health and lifestyle.

- A young child, athletic teenager and pregnant woman all need differing quantities of these components.

3 Food needs to provide us with two important things:

1 **Energy** from carbohydrates is released during respiration – essential to keep our bodies working.

2 The **chemicals** (mainly proteins) which are required for **growth** and to **repair** our bodies.

4 You must *digest* your food before you can use it in your body.

- **Digestion** is the process by which **large molecules** of food are **made smaller** until your body can **absorb** them.

- Digestion starts as soon as food enters your mouth, making food small enough to swallow.

- At various points in your digestive system, substances called **enzymes** become involved. These chemicals are **biological catalysts**. They **increase the speed** at which the **chemical reactions** of digestion take place.

5 Most of the *products of digestion* are useful to the body; others are not.

- Blood absorbs the **small, soluble molecules** produced during digestion when they reach the **small intestine**.

- The **blood system** carries them around the body to the cells where they are needed.

- Some of the molecules in your food **do not dissolve** and are **not digested**.

- These **waste materials** pass through your body and are removed as **faeces**. This process is **egestion**.

food enters gut

food molecules getting smaller

digested food absorbed into the bloodstream

undigested food egested

The digestive system

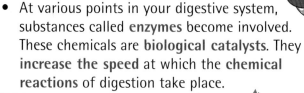

Remember

To stay healthy, everybody needs a balanced diet but this balance is different for different groups.

Copy and complete

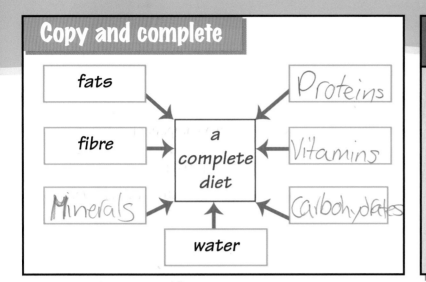

fats → a complete diet ← Proteins

fibre → a complete diet ← Vitamins

Minerals → a complete diet ← Carbohydrates

water →

2 mins

1 How does our body use fibre in our diet?
2 Name three sources of protein in our diet.
3 What are the two most important things that our food provides?
4 What part do enzymes play in the process of digestion?

Questions and model answers

State which of these statements is **true** or **false**. Explain your reason if you think it is false.

1 Elderly people need smaller meals than young adults. True

2 Cucumber is a suitable source of proteins for vegetarians. False. Cucumber is a watery vegetable and contains little protein.

3 Carbohydrates and fats are good sources of energy. True

4 All vegetables must be cooked well before eating. False. They must be washed before eating but salads and lightly cooked vegetables provide us with important vitamins, which can be destroyed by over-cooking.

Comments

Read all of the statements very carefully before deciding which ones are false. There is a good chance that roughly half of the statements in a question of this sort will be true and the other half false.

Make sure your reasoning does not just repeat the words in the question. If you were asked to explain why part one is true, you might say that elderly people are less active than young adults and do not need so much of the bulky energy-providing foods, like potatoes and rice.

Now try these!

The table shows the recommended daily intake of energy and some of the nutrients needed by different groups of people.

| group of people | energy | nutrients (g) | | | minerals (mg) | |
		protein	carbohydrate	fat	calcium	iron
male 15–18	11510	55.2	360	109	1000	11.3
female 15–18	8830	45.0	276	84	800	14.8
male 19–50	10600	55.5	331	100	700	8.7
female 19–50	8100	45.0	254	77	700	14.8
pregnant female	8900	81.0	278	84	700	14.8

1a Explain why two 16 year-old males of the same weight might need different amounts of energy. *(1 mark)*

b Which **two** types of nutrient provide most of the energy in our diet? *(1 mark)*

2a Calculate the difference (in mg) in the recommended daily intake of calcium for a 15 year-old male and a 30 year-old male. *(1 mark)*

b Calcium is needed for healthy bones. Explain the difference in the amount of calcium needed each day by a 15 and a 30 year-old male. *(1 mark)*

The skeleton and movement

1 The skeleton is a system of *bones* and other *soft tissues, ligaments, muscles* and *tendons*, which are all linked together.

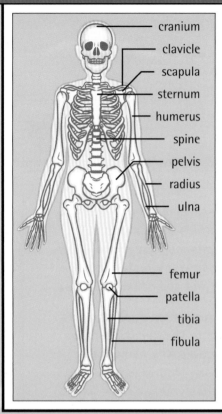

- cranium
- clavicle
- scapula
- sternum
- humerus
- spine
- pelvis
- radius
- ulna
- femur
- patella
- tibia
- fibula

The human skeleton has **three main functions**, it:

- supports the body
- protects vital organs
- allows the body to move.

2 There are several structures and tissues that are important in allowing the body to move.

Joints are points in the skeleton where **two bones meet**. Here are the names and examples of the three types of joint:

type of joint	example
immovable	between bones of skull
slightly movable	between vertebrae of the spine
freely movable	between humerus and scapula

Joints are given names that **describe their function**. Here are some examples of different joints:

action	example
hinge joint	knee, elbow
ball and socket joint	shoulder, hip
sliding joint	wrist

3 Our skeleton is also made up of:

Ligaments are the tough, fibrous and slightly stretchy tissues that hold the bones together at each joint. They prevent the joint from dislocating.

Tendons are strong, non-stretchy tissues that attach muscles to bones. If tendons are damaged then the muscles to which they are attached will not operate fully and moving that part of the body will be difficult and possibly painful.

Muscles are the strong, stretchy tissues that can contract and pull two bones together. They cannot push bones apart. This has to be done by another muscle pulling the bones in the opposite direction as the first muscle relaxes. The pair of muscles moving the bones in opposite directions on either side of a joint is called an antagonistic pair of muscles.

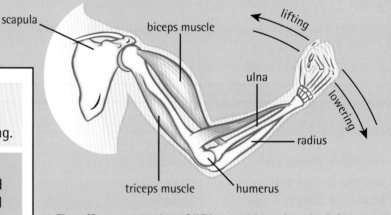

The effect on muscles of lifting and lowering the left arm

Remember

You can only move because of the action of antagonistic muscle pairs acting in either side of the joint, between two bones.

Copy and complete

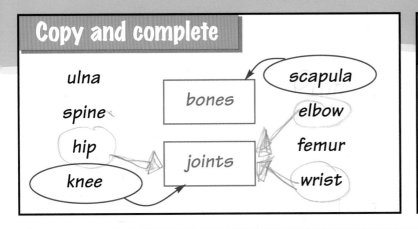

ulna
spine
hip
knee

bones

joints

scapula
elbow
femur
wrist

1 Name two organs that are protected by the rib cage.

2 What is the function of ligaments?

3 What sort of tissues are tendons?

Question and model answer

Describe the action of an antagonistic pair of muscles.

The pair of muscles moving a bone in opposite directions on either side of a joint is called an antagonistic muscle pair. Muscles can only contract to pull bones together. They cannot push bones apart. The bones have to be pulled apart by another muscle acting in the opposite direction as the first muscle relaxes. To allow the joint to move, a pair of muscles acting in opposite directions (antagonistic) is needed.

Comments

There will be several marks for this question, each one awarded for making a particular point in your answer. The three points you will need to make for full marks are:

1 Describe what you understand to be an antagonistic muscle pair.

2 State that muscles can only actively contract and pull towards their centre.

3 Explain that because of this a pair of muscles working in opposite directions is needed at a joint to allow it to move.

Now try these!

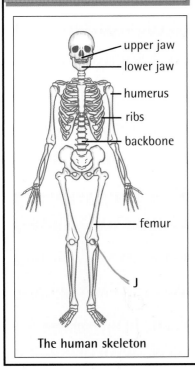

The human skeleton

upper jaw
lower jaw
humerus
ribs
backbone
femur
J

1a Draw a line from the letter **J** to **one** joint in the leg. *(1 mark)*

  b Why do we need joints in our skeleton? *(1 mark)*

2a Which part of our skeleton, labelled in the diagram, moves so that we can breathe? *(1 mark)*

  b Which part of our skeleton, labelled in the diagram, moves so that we can chew? *(1 mark)*

  c Which **one** of the following is needed in the diet for strong bones and teeth? Tick the correct box. *(1 mark)*

aluminium ☐ copper ☐ calcium ☑ iron ☐

The diagram shows part of an arm.

3a Parts A and B are attached to bones. What name is given to parts of the body like parts A and B? *(1 mark)*

  b Part A gets shorter. In which direction does the lower arm move? *(1 mark)*

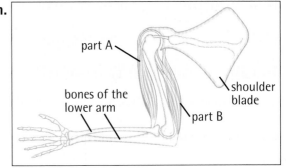

part A
bones of the lower arm
shoulder blade
part B

Respiration

 1 Aerobic respiration involves a reaction in cells between oxygen and food, during which glucose is broken down into carbon dioxide and water.

- In order for humans to **release energy from food**, a supply of oxygen is needed for aerobic respiration to take place.
- Aerobic means 'in the presence of oxygen'.

 3 Gas exchange of carbon dioxide and oxygen occurs in the alveoli.

- **Oxygen** from the air **dissolves** in the surface moisture of the alveoli and passes into the blood stream.
- At the same time carbon dioxide in the blood passes out through the moist surface into the alveoli.
- The air then passes back along the same route and is breathed out through the mouth and nose.

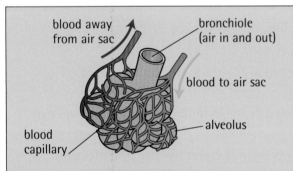

blood away from air sac

bronchiole (air in and out)

blood to air sac

alveolus

blood capillary

Air sacs and their blood supply

 2 Oxygen is obtained from the air that you breathe through your mouth and nose.

- The air passes down the **trachea** (windpipe), which divides into two tubes, called **bronchi**. Each of these is connected to one **lung**.
- Inside each lung, the bronchi divide into many narrower tubes (**bronchioles**) and at the end of each bronchiole is an **air sac**.
- These air sacs are called **alveoli**.
- These have a very **large surface area** which is very **thin**, **moist** and has a **good supply of blood vessels**.

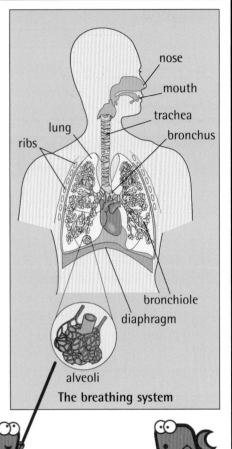

nose

mouth

trachea

lung

bronchus

ribs

bronchiole

diaphragm

alveoli

The breathing system

4 Aerobic respiration can be summarised by this word equation:

glucose + oxygen $\xrightarrow[\text{released}]{\text{energy}}$ carbon dioxide + water

 5 The reactants and products of respiration are transported throughout the body in the bloodstream.

Oxygen is carried around the body in the blood system. Once it reaches the cells where it is needed it can react with the food molecules produced by digestion to release energy.

Remember

During aerobic respiration, glucose (a carbohydrate) reacts with oxygen to release energy, with the production of carbon dioxide and water.

Copy and complete

Aerobic respiration

reactants	products	releasing
_____	carbon dioxide	_____
oxygen	glucose	Water+carbon dioxide

1 What is at the end of the narrow tubes, called bronchioles?
2 Which gas is needed for aerobic respiration to take place?
3 Where does the reaction between glucose and oxygen take place?

Question and model answer

Look at the information in the table:

	% inhaled air	% exhaled air
nitrogen	78	78
oxygen	20.96	17
carbon dioxide	0.04	4
noble gases	1%	1%

Describe and explain the differences between inhaled and exhaled air.

The differences are:

• there is more carbon dioxide in exhaled air
• there is less oxygen in exhaled air.

Respiration uses oxygen and produces carbon dioxide. During breathing, oxygen is removed from inhaled air and carbon dioxide is added to exhaled air.

The amount of nitrogen stays the same.

Comments

In this sort of question you must check the contents of the table carefully. Where the numbers are the same for both inhaled and exhaled air there is no difference. The only two percentage differences are for oxygen and carbon dioxide. Between breathing in and out the percentage of oxygen has decreased and the percentage of carbon dioxide has increased.

Now try these!

The diagram below shows part of the respiratory system.

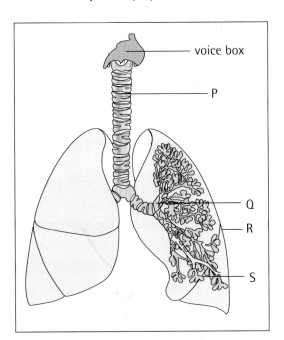

voice box —
P —
Q —
R —
S —

1 From the diagram, give the letters which label:
a the trachea *(1 mark)* P
b alveoli *(1 mark)* S
2 a Which gas passes into the blood from the alveoli? *(1 mark)*
b Which gas passes out of the blood into the alveoli? *(1 mark)*
3 The walls of the capillaries and the alveoli are very thin. Why do they need to be thin? *(2 marks)*
4 There are millions of alveoli in the lungs. They provide a very large surface area. Why is a large surface area necessary? *(2 marks)*

Human reproduction

1 Reproduction in humans is a sexual process.

- Specialised cells, called **gametes**, from two parents are required: one **male** and one **female**.
- The male gamete is the **sperm** and the female gamete is the **ovum** (egg).

3 Changes during adolescence

boys	girls	both
bodies become more muscular	hips widen	experience emotional changes, e.g. insecurity, greater independence, heightened sexual awareness
voice breaks	periods begin	
hair grows on face, chest and armpits	hair grows in armpits	
pubic hair grows	pubic hair grows	
penis becomes larger	breasts develop	hormones that are released into the blood cause these changes

2 Changes occur during puberty.

In boys, puberty occurs between the ages of 12 and 16, when the **testes** start to produce sperm.

When girls reach puberty, the **ovaries** start to release ova between the ages of 11 and 15.

During **adolescence**, which follows puberty, many changes occur to the bodies of boys and girls.

4 The menstrual cycle

- Ova develop in the ovaries of a woman.
- Each month an ovum is released from one of the ovaries, this is called **ovulation**.
- During ovulation, the **lining of the uterus** thickens due to a **greater supply of blood**.
- If it does not meet a sperm, the ovum and the lining of the uterus break down and pass out of the vagina during the woman's monthly bleeding period.
- This process, which takes place about once every 28 days, is called **menstruation**.

5 Fertilisation

- If sperm are released from the penis during sexual intercourse they swim into the uterus.
- They may meet an ovum as they swim towards the ovary along the oviduct.
- Fertilisation takes place if the nucleus of one sperm successfully joins with the nucleus of an ovum.

- The new individual has now started to develop and the woman is pregnant.
- The fertilised ovum then begins to divide into a ball of cells called the embryo, which attaches itself to the lining of the uterus and grows as the cells continue to divide.

6 Development and birth

After 7–8 weeks, the organs of the body begin to develop and the **fetus**, as it is now called, is attached to the **placenta** by the **umbilical cord**.

In the placenta, the blood vessels of the fetus are close to those of the mother.

The umbilical cord allows movement of substances to and from the fetus. **Food** and **oxygen** pass from the mother's blood into that of the fetus. **Carbon dioxide** and other **waste products** pass from the fetus's blood supply into that of the mother.

After about nine months of development inside its mother's womb, the baby is born through the vagina.

Remember

Human reproduction is a sexual process, needing gametes from two parents: one male and one female.

Copy and complete

adolescence	→	The changes are _____ _____ _____
ovulation	→	An ovum is _____ _____ _____
fertilisation	→	A sperm _____ _____ _____

2 mins

1 Which organ produces sperm?
2 Which organ releases the ova?
3 What is the usual length of the menstrual cycle?

Question and model answer

In which ways are the male and female human reproductive systems similar?

The reproductive systems of males and females are totally different. They have specific organs to produce eggs and enable the embryo to develop (female), and to produce sperm (male). The female system is completely internal. The penis and testes hang outside the male body because the penis must be placed inside the vagina during sexual intercourse. The position of the testes means they are cooler than the rest of the body, as sperm cannot survive for long at normal body temperature.

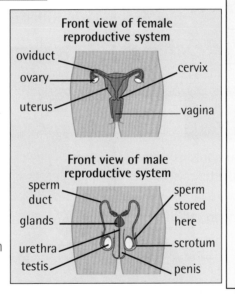

Front view of female reproductive system
- oviduct
- ovary
- uterus
- cervix
- vagina

Front view of male reproductive system
- sperm duct
- glands
- urethra
- testis
- sperm stored here
- scrotum
- penis

Comment

Look carefully at the diagrams in the question before you start answering the question. Write your answer in several short sentences — that way you'll make sure that you describe each difference in turn. Don't assume there are any similarities between the two reproductive systems just because you are asked for them. Explain what you see in the diagrams, based on what you know about this topic.

Now try these!

The diagram shows a baby growing in its mother's uterus.

1a What is the function of the amniotic fluid? *(1 mark)*

b Through which part can harmful substances, such as nicotine, pass from the mother's blood to the baby's blood? *(1 mark)*

c Give **one** other harmful substance which may be passed from the mother's blood to the baby's blood. *(1 mark)*

2 When the baby is born it is pushed out of the mother's body. What happens in the uterine wall to push the baby out? *(1 mark)*

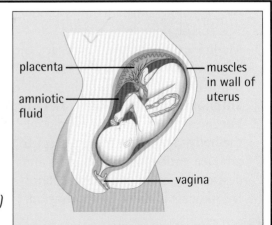

- placenta
- amniotic fluid
- muscles in wall of uterus
- vagina

Staying healthy

1 *Smoking has these long-term effects on health.*

- **Smoke damages the alveoli** in the lungs, making it harder to breathe.

- Tar from the burning tobacco is deposited in the lungs, where **chemicals in the tar can cause lung cancer**.

- **Nicotine** from burning tobacco can **cause high blood pressure**, which damages arteries and strains the heart.

- **Carbon monoxide** in smoke **reduces the amount of oxygen** carried by the blood.

2 *All drugs, including those in cigarette smoke, affect the ways in which the brain and the nervous system work.*

- Many drugs are medicines which, when they are used properly, **prevent** or **treat disease**.

- Any drug (such as those shown below) that is misused can cause physical damage to the body and cause personal and social problems.

- Large quantities of **alcohol will slow down the action of the drinker's brain** making them clumsy, slow to react and have difficulty in making decisions. Continued abuse of alcohol over a long period will result in **damage to the liver and the brain**.

- Drugs, such as heroin and cocaine, can have particularly rapid effects on health with large doses often causing death.

3 *Organisms that cause disease are called pathogens.*

- **Bacteria and viruses** are micro-organisms that cause many infectious diseases. Bacteria (see photo) cause cholera, typhoid, tuberculosis and syphilis. Viruses cause influenza, polio, German measles and AIDS.

- The human body has **natural defences**. Sometimes, however, the body needs extra help to resist the effects of pathogens and to destroy the poisonous substance they produce. This can be done in two ways:

1 **Medicines** can be taken to attack the bacteria that cause the disease. Unfortunately, these medicines, called **antibiotics**, do not affect viruses.

2 **Vaccines** can be given to encourage the body's natural defence system to produce antibodies, which resist and destroy the cause of the infection. This process is called **immunisation**.

Remember

As a fetus develops inside the uterus it is vulnerable to the effects of poisons in its mother's blood stream. Pregnant mothers who smoke have tar and nicotine in their blood that is passed to the fetus. They also have less oxygen in their blood. Women who smoke during pregnancy give birth to smaller babies than those who do not smoke.

Copy and complete

Smoke *damages* _____

Carbon dioxide
reduces _____

Tar *contains* _____

Nicotine *causes* _____

1 *What is a pathogen?*
2 *Name two diseases caused by bacteria.*
3 *Name two diseases caused by viruses.*
4 *What sorts of medicines can attack bacteria?*

Question and model answer

Why is it important to store food properly?

If our food is not stored properly and is exposed to bacteria it can become harmful to us when we eat it. Salting, pickling, canning and drying are all ways that food has been, and still is, stored so that it can be eaten some time after it has been prepared. Each of these processes prevents bacteria from reaching the food or, in the case of pickling, keeps the food in an environment in which the bacteria cannot survive.

Comments

Bacteria exist in the air all the time. If they land on our food they can multiple and look like patches of 'mould'. Keeping food in the refrigerator will slow down the growth of bacteria but will not kill them. Keeping food in a freezer stops the growth of bacteria but does not kill them. Only cooking it properly will kill harmful bacteria in food.

Now try these!

One evening Jenny and Leah ate chicken sandwiches which had been in their school bags all day. There were harmful bacteria in their food. The next day both girls became very ill. Their doctor gave them antibiotics to take for eight days.

1 Use the graph to explain why the girls did not become ill until the day after eating the sandwiches. *(1 mark)*

2 After taking the antibiotics for eight days Jenny was completely better. Explain why she got better. *(1 mark)*

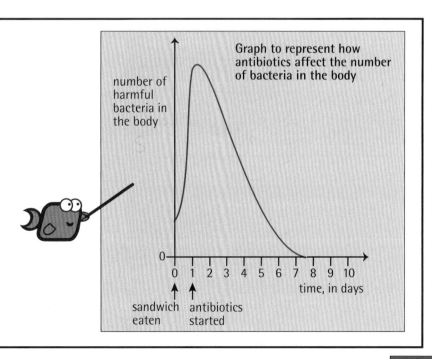

Graph to represent how antibiotics affect the number of bacteria in the body

number of harmful bacteria in the body

time, in days

sandwich eaten

antibiotics started

Photosynthesis

1 Photosynthesis is the chemical reaction by which plants produce biomass for growth.

- **Carbon dioxide** and **water** are the reactants in this reaction.
- **Glucose** (a type of sugar) is the main product of the reaction and **oxygen** is produced as a waste product.
- Glucose is used by the plant to make other compounds that it uses for **growth**.
- Most of the oxygen is released into the atmosphere, which other living things use.

2 Light is required for photosynthesis to take place.

- Light is captured by the green pigment called **chlorophyll**, which is contained within structures called **chloroplasts**.
- Only cells with chloroplasts can photosynthesise. This is because chloroplasts (shown below) contain chlorophyll, which captures light.
- Without light the cell does not have enough energy for photosynthesis to take place.

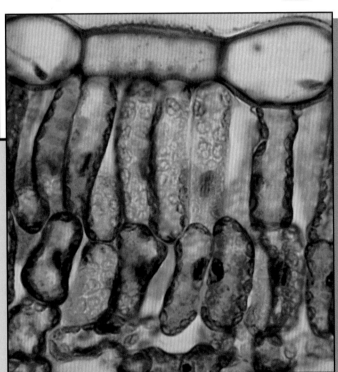

3 Photosynthesis can be summarised in this *word equation*:

carbon dioxide + water $\xrightarrow{\text{light}}$ glucose + oxygen

4 A balanced symbol chemical equation for photosynthesis:

$$6CO_2 + 6H_2O \longrightarrow C_6H_{12}O_6 + 6O_2$$

carbon dioxide + water $\longrightarrow$ glucose + oxygen
(6 lots)   (6 lots)   (1 lot)   (6 lots)

Remember

Photosynthesis is a vital chemical process by which plants make biomass for growth from carbon dioxide and water. This requires light energy. It takes place in the green parts of all plants.

Copy and complete

photosynthesis . . .

. . . uses
1 _____
2 _____

. . . needs
1 _____

. . . produces
1 _____
2 _____

2 mins

1 What is the name of the green pigment that captures light for photosynthesis?
2 Which part of plant cells contains the green pigment?
3 What happens to most of the oxygen produced during photosynthesis?

Question and model answer

Why do plants not give off oxygen at night-time?

As it is dark, no light is available as an energy source for photosynthesis so the reaction does not take place. No oxygen is produced by the reaction so there is none to release into the atmosphere.

Comment

This question asks you to explain why something does not happen, which means that the conditions needed for the production and release of oxygen are not present. It would not be enough to just say that photosynthesis is not taking place; you must explain why it is not taking place and how this prevents the release of oxygen at night-time.

Now try these!

The drawing shows part of a blackberry plant.

1 Photosynthesis takes place in the leaves of the blackberry plant. Complete the word equation for photosynthesis. *(1 mark)*

water + carbon dioxide ⟶ _____ + oxygen

2 Jonathon studied a blackberry plant growing in a shady place and a blackberry plant growing in a sunny place.

a Jonathon found that the plant in the shady place had larger leaves. Why is it an advantage for plants in the shade to have leaves with a large surface area? *(1 mark)*

b Both blackberry plants had green leaves. What part of the leaf cells makes the leaf green? *(1 mark)*

Plant growth

1 Respiration is a chemical reaction between glucose and oxygen that *releases energy* as well as producing *carbon dioxide* and *water*.

- This energy is used by the plant for its life processes. Plants need this energy to:
  1 grow
  2 take up minerals from the soil
  3 move
  4 make specialised cells.

- Some of the oxygen that plants produce during photosynthesis is used in respiration.

3 Plants also need other elements for healthy growth, such as *nitrogen*, *phosphorus* and *potassium*.

- Nitrogen is absorbed from the soil, mainly in the form of **nitrates** dissolved in water that is **absorbed through the roots**.

- Roots also absorb potassium and phosphorus.

- When plants (e.g. the phosphorous-deficient tomato plant below) lack these minerals, their growth is restricted. They are more likely to get diseases and the quantity and quality of the fruit produced is reduced.

- Farmers and gardeners often add fertilisers to the soil to avoid these problems.

2 Respiration involving oxygen is called *aerobic respiration*.

This can be summarised in this word equation:

$$\text{glucose} + \text{oxygen} \xrightarrow[\text{released}]{\text{energy}} \text{carbon dioxide} + \text{water}$$

4 Water is essential for plants and they absorb it from the soil.

- Plant roots have cells at their surface, specially adapted to absorb water and dissolved minerals in the soil.

- These root hair cells have a long hair-like structure, which comes out from the cell body. These provide a very large surface area that is used to absorb water and dissolved mineral salts from the soil.

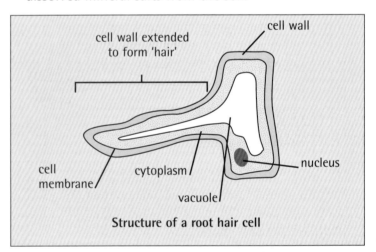

Structure of a root hair cell

Aerobic respiration is the process by which plants produce the energy they need for their life processes.

Copy and complete

aerobic respiration. . .

. . . uses

1 _____

2 _____

. . . produces

1 _____

2 _____

. . . releases

1 _____

2 mins

1 Name three elements needed by plants for healthy growth.
2 Which substances do gardeners and farmers often add to the soil?
3 Which cells absorb water and dissolved salts from the soil?

Question and model answer

How do farmers maintain and improve the quality of crops they grow in their fields?

As they grow, plants use minerals from the soil, which are essential for their growth. There are two ways of replacing these minerals. The first is to grow plants in rotation, including some that add these minerals into the soil. The second is to spread fertilisers (substances that contain these minerals) on the fields.

Comments

Plants need minerals for healthy growth.
Nitrogen is needed for making proteins for good leaf growth. Potassium and phosphorus are important for bud and root growth.
Organic fertilisers (manure and compost) are made from the remains of living things.
Inorganic fertilisers contain minerals and are made from chemicals in factories.

Simply stating 'adding fertilisers' will not get all of the marks for this question. You will have to show that you understand the difference between organic and inorganic fertilisers, in terms of what they are made of and where they come from.

Now try this!

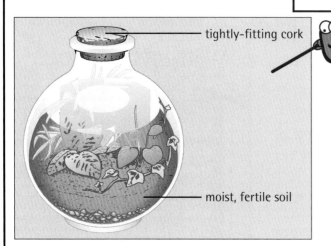

tightly-fitting cork

moist, fertile soil

The drawing shows a bottle garden which is kept in a brightly-lit room.

The cork in the neck of the bottle is not taken out. The plants in the bottle use oxygen for respiration.

Explain why, over one week, the amounts of oxygen and carbon dioxide in the bottle stay about the same. *(3 marks)*

Variation

1 There are many different living things.

- A group of living things that have many similar features and that can successfully interbreed is called a **species**.

- Different species have different features. For example, cats are one species and dogs are another. So, there is **also variation between different species**.

2 Individuals within a species may show *variation*.

Individuals show a range of features that they share with all other members of that species, however, there are differences specific to individuals, called **variations**. For example, human beings have two legs, a skeleton and a nose between two eyes but we don't all have the same eye colour, facial features or body shape.

The causes of variation between members of the same species can be either **inherited** or **environmental**.

3 Inherited causes of variation

- Offspring look more or less like one or both of their parents.

- Human children inherit certain **characteristics** from their parents, such as eye colour, hair colour, nose and ear shape.

- All offspring of any living thing inherit this **genetic information** from one or more of its parents.

- In most animals this can make every individual different from every other individual.

- In some plants this can make all of the offspring exactly the same as the parent plant.

4 Environmental causes of variation

- The information that offspring inherit from their parents is not the only thing that decides the characteristics of an individual. The conditions in which the offspring grow up will also have an effect.

- If a human child has two tall parents and inherits the potential to be tall, they could still turn out to be quite short if they do not eat a **well-balanced diet**.

- The way a child is **brought up, what they eat,** the **education** they receive and the amount of exercise they take can all have an effect on the appearance and characteristics of that child when fully grown.

Variation describes the differences between living things. There are inherited (genetic) causes and environmental causes of variation.

Copy and complete

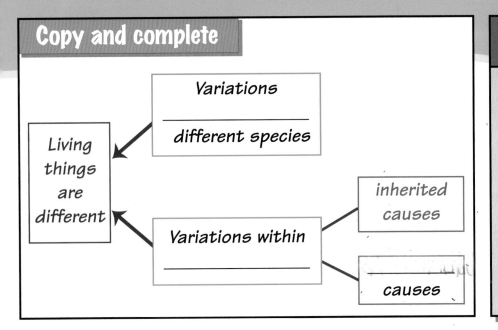

Variations
_____
different species

Living things are different

Variations within
_____

inherited causes

_____
causes

1 What is a species?
2 Name two features that a child might inherit from one of its parents.
3 Name two environmental factors that will affect how tall a child grows.

Questions and model answers

Think of three differences between you and one of your friends.

1 One which has an environmental cause.

    The way you speak and your ability to play a particular game have environmental causes.

2 One which has an inherited cause.

    Your blood group or your eye colours have an inherited cause.

3 One which is caused by both inherited and environmental factors.

    Height and intellect are caused by a combination of environmental and inherited factors.

Comments

To get the correct answers to this question, it is important to ensure that you are clear about the difference between inherited causes and environmental causes of variation. Only features that can be passed on from parents to their children are inherited causes.

Anything in the environment that can affect an individual as it grows and develops can cause variation between that individual and others of the same species.

Now try this!

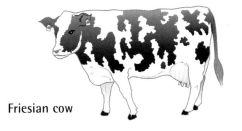

Hereford cow

Friesian cow

Herefords and Friesians are two breeds of cattle. Herefords produce high quality meat. Friesians produce lots of milk. The drawings above show a Hereford cow and a Friesian cow.

1a The **two** breeds of cattle are different in appearance from each other. What causes the variation between them? *(1 mark)*

  b Suggest **two** environmental factors that can affect the amount of meat or milk cattle produce. *(2 marks)*

Classification

1 All living things can be sorted into groups. This process is called *classification*.

- The members of each group have **similar features**.
- A group of living things that have many similar features and that can **successfully interbreed** is called a **species**.

2 All living things on the Earth can be classified into *five kingdoms*:

- the **animal kingdom**
- the **plant kingdom**
- **prokaryotes** (which include bacteria)
- **protoctista** (single-celled animals)
- **fungi**.

HELP!

You need to know about the first two of these: the plant kingdom and the animal kingdom.

3 The plant kingdom

- The first two large groups within this kingdom are plants that **produce seeds** and those that **do not produce seeds**.
- The plants that produce seeds belong to one of two groups – either **flowering plants** or **conifers**.

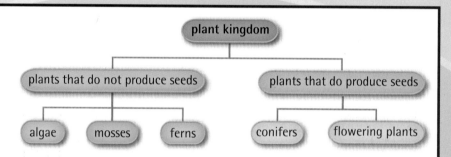

plant kingdom

plants that do not produce seeds → algae, mosses, ferns

plants that do produce seeds → conifers, flowering plants

4 The animal kingdom

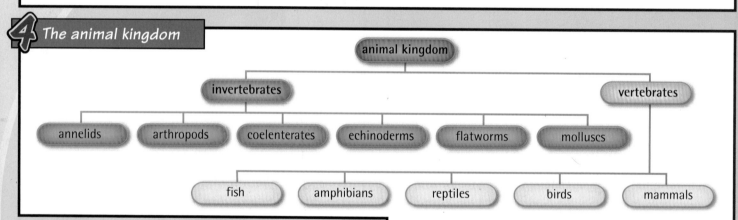

animal kingdom

invertebrates: annelids, arthropods, coelenterates, echinoderms, flatworms, molluscs

vertebrates: fish, amphibians, reptiles, birds, mammals

- The first feature that divides members of the animal kingdom is whether or not the animal has a backbone.
- Animals that have a backbone are called **vertebrates** and animals that do not have a backbone are called **invertebrates**.
- Humans can be classified as:

  animals → vertebrates → mammals

5 Vertebrates all have a *backbone* and each group of vertebrates has features that are *specific to that group*.

- The following features can be used when we try to classify a vertebrate:

group	features they have in common
amphibians	live on land and in water, smooth damp skin and lay soft eggs in water
birds	feathers and lay hard-shelled eggs on land
fish	fins, gills and scales
mammals	hair or fur and feed young on mother's milk
reptiles	hard, dry scales and lay soft-shelled eggs on land

Remember

All living things can be sorted into groups, according to their features.

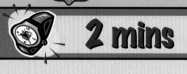

Copy and complete

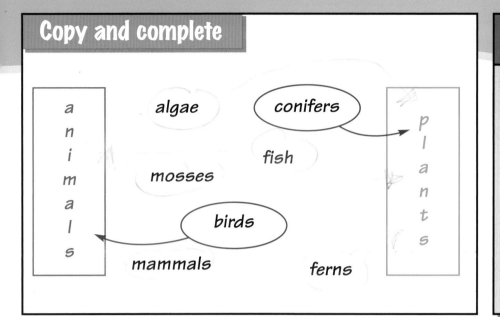

1 How many different kingdoms are there to classify all of the living things on Earth?
2 Name the two groups of plants which produce seeds.
3 What is an invertebrate?

Question and model answer

It is hard to tell the difference between a reptile and an amphibian. What specific features of each help you tell them apart?

Amphibians have smooth, moist skin but reptiles have dry scales.

Amphibians lay their eggs in water but reptiles lay their eggs on land.

Comment

Make sure you say what the difference is (e.g. amphibians lay their eggs in water) and what this is different from (reptiles lay their eggs on land).

Now try these!

Each of the animals in the drawings below belongs to a different group.

1 Write the name of the group the animal belongs to. Choose names from the list below. *(1 mark)*

amphibians   crustaceans   insects   mammals   molluscs   reptiles

a   b   c   d

2 Which of the animals drawn above are invertebrates? Give the correct letters. *(2 marks)*

a + c

Inheritance

1 A chemical called *deoxyribonucleic acid (DNA)*, found inside the nucleus of every cell, carries the *instructions for inherited features*.

- DNA is arranged into coils called **chromosomes**.
- All human cells, except gametes, contain **46 chromosomes**.
- The chromosomes pair up in the nucleus – you have **23 pairs of chromosomes**.
- Gametes contain only one chromosome from each pair – **23 single chromosomes** in total.

2 Along every chromosome are *sets of information*, **called** *genes*.

- Each gene contains the information needed to make one small part of a human being.
- When an **ovum is fertilised by a sperm**, the chromosomes from the sperm nucleus pair up with the chromosomes in the ovum.
- Half of the chromosomes in the cells of the fetus are inherited from the mother and the other half from the father.

3 The developing fetus has two copies of each gene – one copy for each chromosome.

- **Both genes contain the information** needed to make each body part.
- The information in each of the two genes can be **identical** or **slightly different** because one version comes from the mother and the other from the father.

4 There are several versions of eye colour gene that can be inherited.

- One version makes blue eyes and another version makes brown eyes.
- A fetus could inherit a gene for brown eyes from its mother and a gene for blue eyes from its father. What colour eyes will the baby actually have? The baby will have brown eyes because **some versions of genes are more powerful than others**.
- This is because the **gene for brown eyes is dominant**.
- The **gene for blue eyes is recessive**. It is overpowered by the dominant gene for brown eyes.

5 For many hundreds of years, farmers have used knowledge of *inheritance* to *develop particular characteristics* in farm animals and plants.

- If a farmer wanted to improve the quality of the wool produced by his sheep, he would choose a ram (male) and ewe (female) that **both have the desired quality of wool** and breed from them.
- The offspring from this pair that have the best quality wool would then be chosen to breed from. The offspring from these parents, also having the desired quality of wool, would be used to breed from in the same way.
- In each new generation, over many years, this particular characteristic will be bred into the sheep. This is called **selective breeding**.
- Farmers decide which characteristics they want a particular animal or plant to have and choose animals or plants with those characteristics to breed from. The same is true of all farm animals and crops that farmers produce today.
- Characteristics, such as rapid weight gain in pigs and the size and flavour of apples, can be 'bred for' in the same way.

Remember

All offspring inherit features which are a result of the genes they receive from each of their parents.

Copy and complete

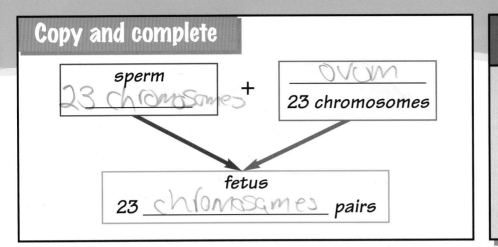

sperm
23 chromosomes

+

ovum
23 chromosomes

fetus
23 chromosomes pairs

2 mins

1 How are chromosomes arranged in the nucleus?
2 What is a recessive gene?
3 What chemical name is DNA short for?

Question and model answer

Using a genetic cross diagram, what are the possible offspring formed by a mother with black hair (Bb) and a father with blonde hair (bb)?

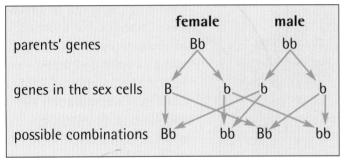

	female	**male**
parents' genes	Bb	bb
genes in the sex cells	B b	b b
possible combinations	Bb bb	Bb bb

A genetic cross diagram shows all of the combinations of genes that are possible at fertilisation.

Two of the four combinations will produce children with black hair (Bb) and the other two combinations will produce children with blonde hair (bb).

Comments

This diagram shows the possible combinations of hair colour of children of a blonde-haired man and black-haired woman. 'B' is the dominant gene for black hair and 'b' is the recessive gene for blonde hair. Each child will always receive a 'b' gene from its father and either a 'B' or 'b' gene from its mother.

Check what each of the letters stands for in the diagram before answering the question. There are four possible outcomes shown in these diagrams but some outcomes may be the same.

Now try these!

The drawing shows a calf produced by mating a Hereford bull with a Friesian cow. Cattle bred in this way will produce both high quality meat and a high milk yield.

1 What term is used to describe this deliberate mating of two different breeds of animals to produce offspring with particular characteristics? *(1 mark)*

2 Farmers want their cattle to produce high quality meat and a high milk yield. Suggest **one** other characteristic which farmers might want their cattle to have. *(1 mark)*

1 The *habitat* of a plant or animal is the place *where it normally lives.*

- Habitats can be very different. Look at the examples below: a freshwater pond, a rocky seashore, dense woodland and desert are all examples of different habitats.

- They differ because some are wet, some are light, some are windy and some have other **conditions particular to them**.

2 Each different habitat has particular groups of plants and animals living in it.

- Each species of plant and animal survives well in the **particular environmental conditions** of that habitat.

- These conditions are **not always constant**. There may be seasonal and even daily changes in these conditions. For example, there could be changes in **temperature**, or in the availability of **water**.

- The plants and animals in a habitat are **adapted to survive these changes**. For example, the canopy produced by the leaves in woodland areas reduces the amount of light that can reach plants on the woodland floor. Without sufficient light, some flowering plants in this habitat would be unable to produce their seeds, so they produce and disperse their seeds before the trees come into leaf.

3 All plants need *light, water* and *space* to survive. All animals need *food, water* and *space* to survive.

- All the members of a species need these same things from their habitat. They have to **compete with each other** to ensure that they each get enough of these things to survive.

- This competition **limits the number of each species** that can survive in a particular habitat.

- If the amounts of water, light or food in the habitat change, then the numbers of a particular species will be affected.

- If a large shrub dies, the amount of light reaching a flowering plant may increase, it can produce more seeds and these will have more room to germinate and to grow.

- If a pond dries up, the number of animals in a habitat will decline because they go elsewhere to drink, or die because of lack of water.

Remember

Living things that compete successfully for resources (light, water, space or food) in the habitat are more likely to reproduce successfully and their offspring are more likely to survive than the offspring of less successful parents.

Work-out!

Copy and complete

There are seasonal and daily **chances** in the environment.

Living things **adapt** to survive.

Species **compele** with each other to obtain the things they need to survive.

2 mins

1 What is a habitat?
2 What do all animals need to survive?
3 What limits the number of each species that can survive in a particular habitat?

Question and model answer

Why do some animals hibernate in harsh habitats?
In some habitats, food may be very scarce during the winter months. In order to conserve energy, these animals slow down their body processes and sleep for many months.

Comments

The question asks you to give the reason why something happens and there is sometimes a clue in the wording. In this case the word 'harsh' points you towards the climate of the habitat. So the correct answers must make the link between the environmental conditions and the shortage of food.

This is an example of how some species of animals are adapted to survive some extreme changes in their habitats.

Now try this!

The drawing shows some of the animals that live at the bottom of the North Sea.

Suggest **two** advantages clams get from living in the sediment. *(2 marks)*

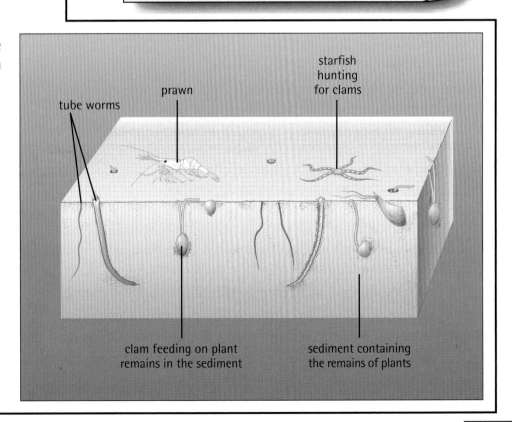

Food webs

1 A number of factors affect populations.

- The **population size** of a particular species in a habitat is affected by the number of other species, called **predators**, which eat it for food.

- The numbers of **herbivores** and **omnivores** that feed on them affects the numbers of a particular plant.

3 The size of the population at each stage in a food chain can be summarised using a diagram called a *pyramid of numbers*.

- Food webs do not give any information about the **numbers of particular plants and animals** that belong to a specific part of the food web or food chain. Instead this is shown in a **pyramid of numbers**.

- The **size of each layer** in the pyramid represents the **numbers of each organism** at that point in the food chain.

- Generally, the number of organisms **decreases** as you go up the pyramid.

2 The feeding relationships in a habitat can be summarised by a *food web*.

- A food web shows the **links between individual food chains** where a producer or consumer is eaten by more than one other consumer.

- Food webs show which organisms eat others for food.

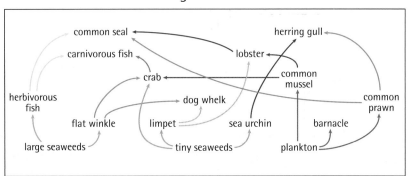

Food chains link together to make a food web

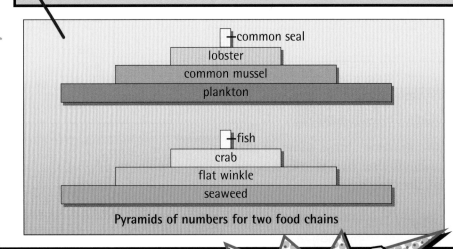

Pyramids of numbers for two food chains

4 There are dangers in the food chain!

- Sometimes **toxic** (poisonous) substances, like insecticides, get into a food chain.
- The plants and animals low down in the food chain are usually unharmed by the **relatively low concentrations** of poison inside them.
- The poison can **become more concentrated** in the bodies of animals further up the food chain.
- Large animals eat many smaller animals so can take in **large quantities of the poison**.
- It may be impossible for the large animals to get rid of the poison. This means that the amount of poison in their bodies builds up until they die from its effects.

Remember

Food webs and pyramids of numbers represent the feeding relationships in a habitat.

Work-out!

Copy and complete

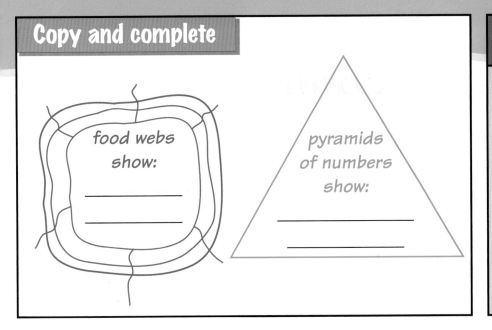

food webs
show:

_____

_____

pyramids
of numbers
show:

_____

_____

2 mins

1 *What affects the numbers of a particular species in a habitat?*

2 *What does the size of each layer in a pyramid of numbers represent?*

3 *Why are animals and plants low down in a food chain usually unharmed by poisons in a food chain?*

Question and model answer

Write a short definition of each of these terms:

carnivore	An animal that eats other animals.
herbivore	An animal that only eats plants.
omnivore	An animal that eats both plants and animals.
producer	An organism, usually a plant, which make its own biomass.
consumer	An organism that feeds on a producer or another consumer.
predator	An animal that kills and eats other animals.
prey	An animal that is killed for food by another animal.

Comment

All of these terms are used in questions that relate to this part of the subject, so you need to undertand them all.

Now try these!

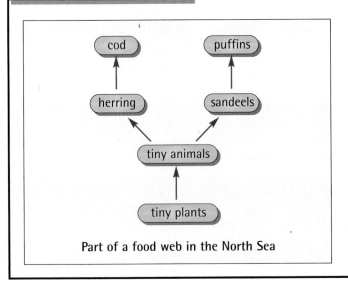

Part of a food web in the North Sea

Herring, sandeels and cod are types of fish. Puffins are sea birds. Herring lay eggs in the gravel on the seabed. Sandeels live where the seabed is covered with sand.

Millions of cubic metres of gravel and sand are removed from the bottom of the North Sea every year for roads and buildings.

1 Give **one** way removing some of the sand and gravel might cause:

- the numbers of herring to decrease *(1 mark)*
- the number of cod to decrease. *(1 mark)*

2 Explain why removing some of the sand has led to a decrease in the number of puffins. *(2 marks)*

KS3 Bitesize Science

States of matter

 1 Every substance is made of a different kind of matter.

- All matter can exist in three states: **solid**, **liquid** and **gas**.
- All substances are:
  - **solids** at temperatures **below** their melting temperature
  - **liquids** at temperatures **between** their melting temperature and their boiling temperature
  - **gases** at temperatures **above** their boiling point.

 2 Here are some examples of substances in solid, liquid and gas state.

	solid	liquid	gas
water	below 0 °C	above 0 °C and below 100 °C	above 100 °C
mercury	below −38 °C	above −38 °C and below 357 °C	above 357 °C

 3 Each state of matter has different properties.

solid	liquid	gas
fixed shape	shape of container	shape of container
difficult to compress	difficult to compress	easy to compress
does not flow	flows easily	flows easily
fixed volume	fixed volume	volume of the container
high density	low density	very low density

 4 The particle theory can be used to explain the properties of the three states of matter.

- The **particle theory** considers all matter as being made up of millions of very small particles.
- The ideas in this particle model can be used to explain the **differences in the properties of the three states of matter**.
- **Solids** have a **fixed shape**, are **hard to compress** and do **not flow**. This is because solids are made up of particles that are in a **fixed regular pattern**, very **close together** and held together by **strong forces**.
- The properties of both liquids and gases can be explained in the same way.

Arrangement of particles in a solid, liquid and a gas			
	solids	**liquids**	**gases**
arrangement of particles	fixed, regular pattern	irregular	irregular
forces between the particles	strong forces	strong forces	very weak forces
movement of the particles	particles vibrate in a fixed position	move freely but quite slowly	very fast and random
distance between particles	very close together	close together	far apart

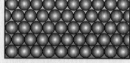 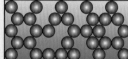 

Everything around us is a solid, a liquid or a gas.

Copy and complete

solids:
- fix shape
- have high density

gases:
- easy to compress
- have very low density

liqid:
- take on shape of container
- diffecit to compless

1 What is the melting temperature of mercury?
2 Which two states of matter flow easily?
3 What is the arrangement of particles in a solid?

Question and model answer

How does the particle theory explain the properties of gases?

Gases have the shape and volume of their container, are easy to compress and flow easily. This is because they are made up of particles, which are moving around very fast at random and are far apart because they have very weak forces between them.

Comments

The particle theory is a very useful set of ideas that helps us to understand the properties of the different states of matter and what happens when a substance changes from one state to another.

There will be several marks for answering a question of this type correctly. You must make sure that your answer refers to the properties of gases and how the particle theory explains each one.

Now try these!

Some crushed ice, at −20 °C, was placed in a beaker. A thermometer was put into the ice, and the beaker was heated gently for 15 minutes.

The graph shows how the reading on the thermometer changed over the 15 minutes.

1 By how much did the temperature in the beaker change during the 15 minutes? *(1 mark)*

2 Which letter on the graph shows:
   a when the ice is melting? *(1 mark)*
   b when the water is boiling? *(1 mark)*

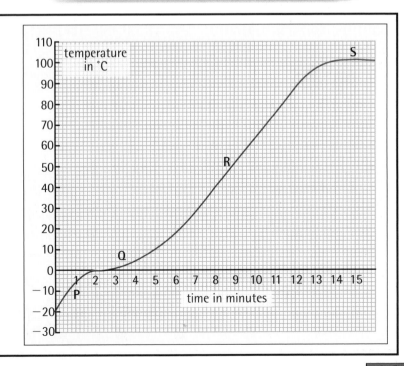

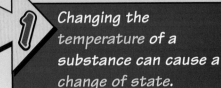

1. Changing the temperature of a substance can cause a change of state.

The particle model can be used to explain what is happening during each of these changes of state.

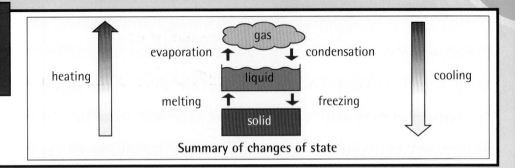

Summary of changes of state

2. One example of a change of state is melting.

- In melting, the **thermal energy** provided to the solid makes the **particles vibrate faster** and more violently until the **forces** holding the particles together break.

- The particles are then able to flow away from the fixed pattern because they have become part of a liquid.

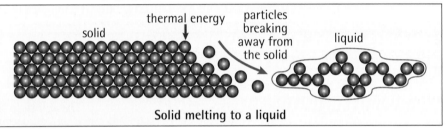

Solid melting to a liquid

3. Another example of a change of state is evaporation.

- The thermal energy provided to the liquid makes the particles move faster.

- Some of the particles close to the surface of the liquid have enough energy to travel upwards to escape from the surface of the liquid into the air above.

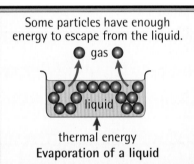

Some particles have enough energy to escape from the liquid.

Evaporation of a liquid

4. The pressure that a gas exerts on the inside of its container is caused by the collisions between the gas particles and the sides of the container.

- The pressure will change if the **number of collisions** changes or the **speed** at which the particles are travelling changes.

- The movement of particles to fill all of the available space or to move between the particles of another substance is called **diffusion**.

- The particles of a smelly substance move away from the substance because particles in the air collide with them and move them about.

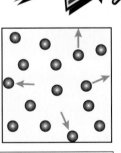

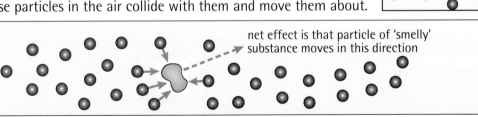

net effect is that particle of 'smelly' substance moves in this direction

Remember

You can use the particle theory to explain the properties of the different states of matter.

Copy and complete

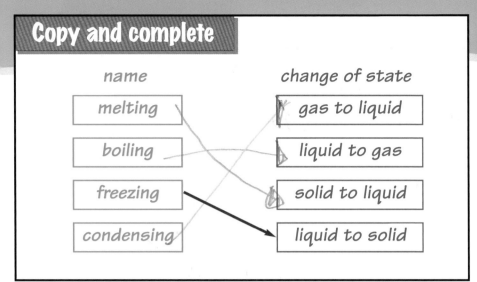

name		change of state
melting		gas to liquid
boiling		liquid to gas
freezing		solid to liquid
condensing		liquid to solid

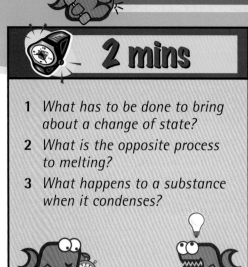

2 mins

1 What has to be done to bring about a change of state?
2 What is the opposite process to melting?
3 What happens to a substance when it condenses?

Question and model answer

Water has a melting point of 0°C and relative density of 1.0. Paraffin wax has a melting point of 60°C and relative density of 0.8.

What **two** things would happen if a piece of paraffin wax was put into a beaker of water heated to 70°C?

The two things that would happen are that:

• the paraffin wax will melt
• the paraffin wax will float on the water.

Comments

In questions like this, the answers will relate to the data you are given. In this question you are given data about two physical properties: melting points and relative density.

The water is hotter than the melting temperature of the paraffin – it will be warmed by the water and melt. Substances with a relative density greater than water sink. Substances with a relative density lower then water float. The relative density of paraffin wax (0.8) is lower than that of water (1.0) so it floats.

Now try these!

This question is about four chemical elements.

1 The melting points and boiling points of the four elements are shown in the table. Complete the table to give the physical state (solid, liquid or gas) of each element at room temperature, 21°C. *(4 marks)*

element	melting point in °C	boiling point in °C	physical state at room temperature, 21°C
bromine	−7	59	liquid
chlorine	−101	−34	gas
fluorine	−220	−188	gas
iodine	114	184	solid

2 Bromine can be a solid, a liquid or a gas depending on the temperature. In which physical state will 10g of bromine store the most thermal energy? *(1 mark)*

3 Is bromine a solid, a liquid or a gas when the arrangement of particles is:

a far apart and random? *(1 mark)*
b close together but random? *(1 mark)*
c close together in a regular pattern? *(1 mark)*

Atoms and molecules

1 All matter is made up of tiny particles called *atoms.*

Each different atom has a different number of protons.

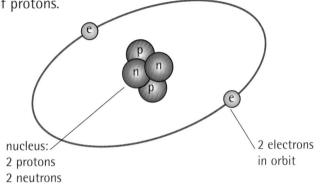

nucleus:
2 protons
2 neutrons

2 electrons
in orbit

Diagram of the components of an atom

2 Atoms consist of *protons* and *neutrons* surrounded by *orbiting electrons.*

Protons and neutrons are:
- packed together in the **nucleus** of the atom
- about the **same size** as each other.

Electrons:
- are **very small** compared to protons and neutrons
- **orbit** around the nucleus.

The **number of protons** in an atom is the same as the number of electrons, and this is called the **atomic number.**

The number of neutrons plus the number of protons is called the **mass number.**

Atoms of the same element may have a **different number of neutrons.** These are called **isotopes** of the element.

3 When two or more atoms are *chemically joined together, they form a molecule. Molecules can be a combination of the same type of atom.*

	formula
A molecule of hydrogen gas is two hydrogen atoms joined together. H H	H_2
A molecule of oxygen gas is two oxygen atoms joined together. O O	O_2

4 Molecules can also be a combination of the atoms of two or more *different elements.*

	formula
A molecule of carbon dioxide is one atom of carbon joined to two atoms of oxygen. O C O	CO_2
A molecule of methane is one atom of carbon joined to four atoms of hydrogen. H H C H H	CH_4

Everything is made up of atoms. Combinations of atoms are called molecules.

Work-out!

Copy and complete

Atoms are
made up of:
neutrons
protons
electrons

combine

→

to make

m <u>olecules</u>

2 mins

1 Which two particles make up
   the nucleus of an atom?
2 What name is given to the
   number of protons in a
   particular atom?
3 What is a molecule?

Question and model answer

Sulphuric acid has the formula H_2SO_4.

What is the total number of atoms in this
molecule and what are they?

The total number of atoms in the molecule is
seven. Of the seven there are two hydrogen,
one sulphur and four oxygen.

Comments

The symbols tell you that there are three
different atoms – H, S and O.

If there are numbers to the bottom right of
the symbol they tell you how many of that
atom are combined in the molecule.

Now try these!

The table gives the numbers of protons,
neutrons and electrons in some atoms of
elements. The letters used in the table are not
the chemical symbols of the elements.

atom	protons	neutrons	electrons
J	16	16	16
L	10	10	10
M	11	12	11
R	17	20	17
Z	17	18	17

Use this information to answer the following questions.

1 Give the letters of:
   a two atoms of the same element
   b an atom or ion with a mass number of 20. *(2 marks)*
2 How many electrons does an atom with an atomic
   number of 16 have? *(1 mark)*
3 What is the atomic number of element M? *(1 mark)*

Elements, compounds and mixtures

1 A substance made up of just one type of atom is called an *element*.

Elements are pure substances that **cannot be split up** into simpler substances.

There are about 100 different known elements.

Elements:

- can be represented by a **symbol** – e.g. C for carbon, O for oxygen

- are all shown in the **periodic table**

- are made up of atoms that all have the **same number of protons**

- have a number in the periodic table, which is the **number of protons** in their atoms

- can chemically combine to form compounds.

Some common elements:

element	symbol	element	symbol
iron	Fe	carbon	C
magnesium	Mg	oxygen	O
calcium	Ca	hydrogen	H
copper	Cu	silicon	Si
titanium	Ti	neon	Ne
tin	Sn	sulphur	S

2 Most of the substances around us contain *more than one element*.

Compounds are substances made up of the atoms of two or more different elements that have joined together during a **chemical reaction**.

Compounds:

- have **chemical properties** that are different to the properties of elements from which they are made

- can be represented by a **formula** – for example, H_2O for water, NaCl for sodium chloride

- are chemical combinations of elements in **fixed proportions**.

The number after the symbol of each element is the number of atoms that combine in that compound.
For example, ethane has the formula C_2H_4, which means that two atoms of carbon combine with four atoms of hydrogen.

3 A *mixture* is a combination of substances that are *not chemically combined*.

- A mixture is different to a compound, in which the different elements are chemically combined.

- The substances that make up mixtures can be **separated** using a wide range of techniques.

Methods of separating mixtures are described on page 44.

Remember

Elements are substances made up of just one type of atom. Every substance on Earth is made from a combination of elements.

Copy and complete

Elements are represented by ___Symbols___.

They are shown in the ___periodic table___.

Atoms have _____.

Atoms combine to form _____.

1 How many different types of atoms are there in all elements?
2 What is the chemical symbol for copper?
3 How many atoms of hydrogen are there in a molecule of ethane?

Question and model answer

Air is a combination of gases at room temperature. These are the chemical formulae for some of the substances in the air – Ar, CO_2, H_2O, N_2, Ne, O_2.

Which of these are:
- atoms of elements? Ar and Ne
- molecules of elements? N_2 and O_2
- compounds? CO_2 and H_2O

Comments

In questions like this, check all of the chemical formulae so that you know how many different substances are contained in the list. Even if you are not familiar with a particular substance, you should be able to work out from the formula, exactly what sort of substance it is.

Elements are single substances. Single atoms of Ar (argon) and Ne (neon) exist in the air. N_2 (nitrogen) and O_2 (oxygen) exist as molecules in the air.
CO_2 (carbon dioxide) and H_2O (water) are compounds – they are made up of more than one element.

Now try these!

The diagrams represent the arrangement of atoms or molecules in four different substances: A, B, C and D.

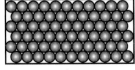

A

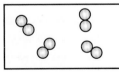

B

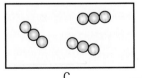

C

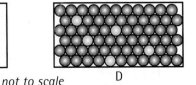

not to scale

D

Each of the circles, ⬤ ◯ ◯, represents an atom of a different element.

1 Which substance is a compound? *(1 mark)*
2 Which substance is a mixture? *(1 mark)*
3 Which **two** substances are elements? *(1 mark)*
4 Which **two** substances could be good thermal conductors? *(1 mark)*
5 Which substance could be carbon dioxide? *(1 mark)*

The periodic table

The periodic table represents all of the known elements arranged in groups according to similar properties.

I ①	II ②											III	IV	V	VI	VII ③	0 ④
																	He Helium 2
Li Lithium 3	Be Beryllium 4											B Boron 5	C Carbon 6	N Nitrogen 7	O Oxygen 8	F Fluorine 9	Ne Neon 10
Na Sodium 11	Mg Magnesium 12											Al Aluminium 13	Si Silicon 14	P Phosphorus 15	S Sulphur 16	Cl Chlorine 17	Ar Argon 18
K Potassium 19	Ca Calcium 20	Sc Scandium 21	Ti Titanium 22	V Vanadium 23	Cr Chromium 24	Mn Manganese 25	Fe Iron 26	Co Cobalt 27	Ni Nickel 28	Cu Copper 29	Zn Zinc 30	Ga Gallium 31	Ge Germanium 32	As Arsenic 33	Se Selenium 34	Br Bromine 35	Kr Krypton 36
Rb Rubidium 37	Sr Strontium 38	Y Yttrium 39	Zr Zirconium 40	Nb Niobium 41	Mo Molybdenum 42	Tc Technetium 43	Ru Ruthenium 44	Rh Rhodium 45	Pd Palladium 46	Ag Silver 47	Cd Cadmium 48	In Indium 49	Sn Tin 50	Sb Antimony 51	Te Tellurium 52	I Iodine 53	Xe Xenon 54
Cs Caesium 55	Ba Barium 56	La Lanthanum 57 X	Hf Hafnium 72	Ta Tantalum 73	W Tungsten 74	Re Rhenium 75	Os Osmium 76	Ir Iridium 77	Pt Platinum 78	Au Gold 79	Hg Mercury 80	Tl Thallium 81	Pb Lead 82	Bi Bismuth 83	Po Polonium 84	At Astatine 85	Rn Radon 86
Fr Francium 87	Ra Radium 88	Ac Actinium 89 •															

H Hydrogen 1

This line divides the metals from the non-metals.

transition metals

x Lanthanide series

	Ce Cerium 58	Pr Praseodymium 59	Nd Neodymium 60	Pm Promethium 61	Sm Samarium 62	Eu Europium 63	Gd Gadolinium 64	Tb Terbium 65	Dy Dysprosium 66	Ho Holmium 67	Er Erbium 68	Tm Thulium 69	Yb Ytterbium 70	Lu Lutetium 71

• Actinide series

	Th Thorium 90	Pa Protactinium 91	U Uranium 92	Np Neptunium 93	Pu Plutonium 94	Am Americium 95	Cm Curium 96	Bk Berkelium 97	Cf Californium 98	Es Einsteinium 99	Fm Fermium 100	Md Mendelevium 101	No Nobelium 102	Lr Lawrencium 103

KEY

```
   X
element name
   Z
```

X = atomic symbol
Z = atomic number

① Group I comprises the alkali metals.

② Group II comprises the alkaline–earth metals.

③ Group VII comprises the halogens.

④ Group 0 comprises the noble gases.

- Elements are arranged in the table in **order of their atomic number**.

- Each box contains the **symbol** for the element, the **name** of the element and its **atomic number**.

- The atomic number of the element is the **number of protons** and the **number of electrons** in the atoms of the element.

Elements with similar properties are grouped together within the periodic table.

- The **most reactive metals** are on the **left** of the table.

- **Non–metals** are on the **right** of the table.

- The metals in the **middle** of the table are called **transition metals**.

- Elements are arranged into **groups, which go down the table**. There are eight groups numbered I to 0 at the top of each column.

- Elements are arranged in **periods, which go across the table**. There are seven periods numbered 1 to 7 down the left side of the table.

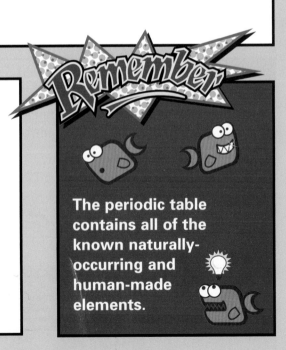

Remember

The periodic table contains all of the known naturally-occurring and human-made elements.

Copy and complete

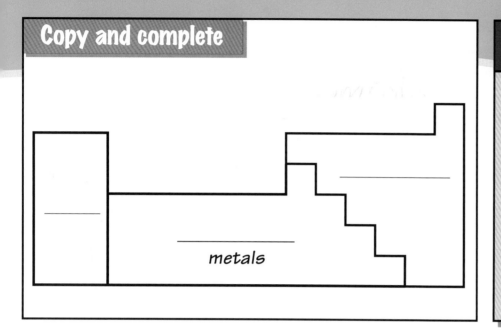

_____

_____

metals

2 mins

1 What is the symbol for lead?
2 What is the name of the element with the symbol W?
3 What is the name of the element with the atomic number of 50?

Question and model answer

Sodium chloride is formed when sodium and chlorine combine together in equal proportions during a chemical reaction.

Write the symbols for:

a sodium Na
b chlorine Cl
c sodium chloride. NaCl

Comments

You need to be familiar with the symbols for the elements that make up the substances you use during your practical work in science. The symbols for both sodium and chlorine can be found in the periodic table.

Combining in equal proportions means that one atom of sodium combines with one atom of chlorine so the formula includes just the symbols for both elements.

Now try these!

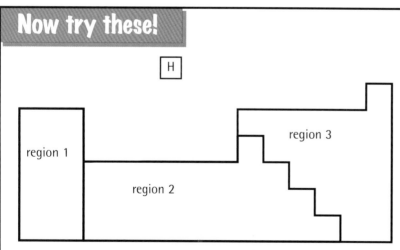

H

region 1

region 2

region 3

The diagram shows an outline of part of the periodic table of elements.

1 What is the name of the element with the symbol H? *(1 mark)*

2 In which regions of the periodic table are the following types of element found:
   a non-metals, e.g. oxygen and chlorine? *(1 mark)*
   b very reactive metals, e.g. sodium and potassium? *(1 mark)*
   c less reactive metals, e.g. copper and zinc? *(1 mark)*

3 Why is copper sulphate not found in the periodic table? *(1 mark)*

Separating mixtures

Mixtures of different substances can be separated in a variety of ways.

The following separation techniques can only be used to separate a mixture of substances that are **not chemically combined**.

Filtration

Separates
Insoluble solids from liquids.

Example
Sand from a sugar solution.

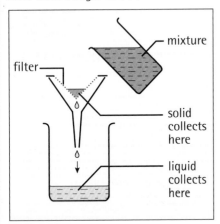

Evaporation

Separates
Soluble solids from their solvent.

Example
Copper sulphate from water.

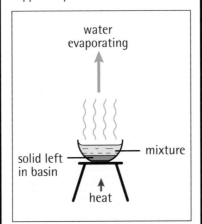

Distillation

Separates
Solids from a liquid or a mixture of liquids.

Example
Vinegar from water.

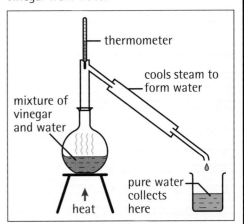

Fractional distillation

Separates: mixtures of liquids with different boiling temperatures.

Example: hydrocarbons in crude oil.

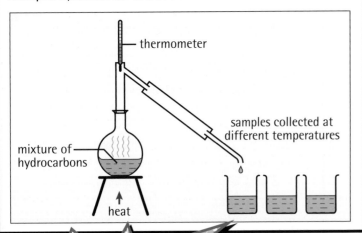

Chromatography

Separates: mixtures of different coloured substances.

Example: different colours in a sample of dye.

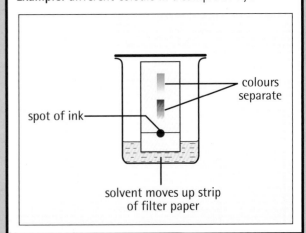

Remember

These physical processes are the means by which substances in a mixture can be separated from each other.

Copy and complete

filtration		soluble solids from their solvents
evaporation		liquids with different boiling temperatures
distillation	*separates*	insoluble solids from liquids
	separates	a mixture of coloured dyes
chromatography		

2 mins

1 What method would be suitable for separating a mixture of sand and salt solution?
2 Which types of substances can be separated using distillation?
3 Which methods of separation rely on the use of thermal energy?

Question and model answer

Sometimes you find white lines around the sides of your shoes. These are often visible the day after you have worn the shoes in the snow and walked on a 'gritted' footpath.

What has caused these white marks on your shoes and how has it happened?

The salt in the grit that has been put on the footpath causes the marks. The salt in the gritting mixture has dissolved in the snow. This has melted and made your shoes wet. Overnight your shoes have dried out; the water has evaporated and left the salt behind on your shoes.

Comment

In questions like this, you will need to read the introduction carefully as it will give you all of the information that you need to understand the type of answer required. There are two parts needed in your answer. First, you have to name the substance responsible for causing the white marks, and, second, you have to explain how it got onto your shoes and how it became visible.

Now try these!

Cathy has two orange drinks: X and Y. She uses chromatography to identify the coloured substances in the drinks. Her experiment is shown below.

Cathy made the chromatogram below using drink X, three food colourings, E102, E160, E110, and drink Y.

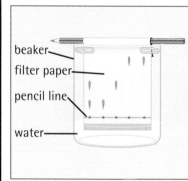

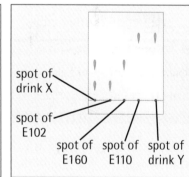

Cathy's chromatogram

1a Use Cathy's chromatogram to identify the two coloured substances in drink X. Write down their E-numbers. *(2 marks)*
  b Draw another spot on Cathy's chromatogram to show what it would look like if drink Y contained E102 as well. *(1 mark)*
  c Chromatography separates the coloured substances in a drink. How can you tell from a chromatogram how many coloured substances there are in a drink? *(1 mark)*
2a The spots show up well on filter paper. Give **one** other reason why filter paper is used in this experiment. *(1 mark)*
  b The line at the bottom of a chromatogram should be drawn with a pencil. Why should the line **not** be drawn with ink? *(1 mark)*

Physical changes

 1 *Physical changes only alter the form and appearance of a substance.*

After a physical change:
- the substance might **look different**
- its **mass** is exactly the **same**
- its **chemical composition** is exactly the **same**.

HELP! **A physical change does not produce a new substance.**

2 *A change of state is one type of physical change.*

- Melting and boiling are both examples of a change of state.
- At room temperature (about 21 °C), oxygen is a gas, water is a liquid and aluminium is a solid. This is because all substances change state at different temperatures.

Here are the melting and boiling temperatures for these three substances:

name	melting temperature °C	boiling temperature °C
oxygen	−218	−183
water	0	100
aluminium	660	2467

 3 *There are other types of physical change.*

- The **form of a solid** can be changed without a change of state – for example, marble rock crushed to marble chips.

- Substances can **expand** or **contract**.
- One substance can **dissolve** in another.

 4 *When one substance dissolves in another, a mixture, called a solution, is formed.*

The dissolved substance is called the **solute** and the substance that it dissolves into is called the **solvent**.

Solutes can be a solid, liquid or gas but they are usually liquids.

Solubility is a measure of **how soluble a substance is in a particular solvent**. It is calculated by finding the maximum mass of the substance that dissolves in 100 g of water at a particular temperature.

A **saturated solution** is when the maximum mass of solute dissolves in a solvent and no more can be dissolved.

The solubility of:
- the same solute in the same solvent is different at different temperatures
- the same solute is different in different solvents
- different solutes at the same temperature is very different.

Insoluble substances can be separated from solutions by **centrifuging** them. This involves spinning a test tube sample round very quickly, which forces the insoluble particles to separate from the rest of the sample.

Remember

After a physical change, a substance may look different but, chemically, it is still the same substance.

Work-out!

Copy and complete

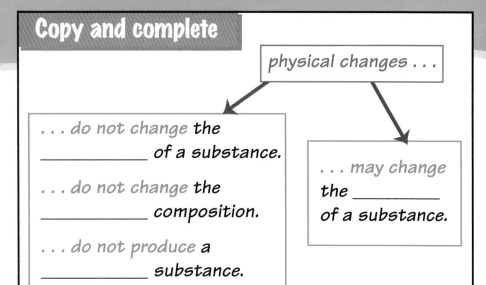

physical changes . . .

. . . do not change **the** _____ of a substance.

. . . do not change **the** _____ composition.

. . . do not produce **a** _____ substance.

. . . may change the _____ of a substance.

 2 mins

1 How is solubility calculated?
2 What is the general name for the substance that dissolves in a solvent?
3 What is a saturated solution?

Question and model answer

Use the particle model to explain what happens when a substance expands.

When most objects are heated they expand (get bigger), and when objects are cooled they contract (get smaller). By supplying thermal energy to the particles of a substance they are able to move further apart. In liquids and gases the particles can move apart freely but even in solids the particles are able to vibrate more vigorously and move further apart. The total effect of the particles moving further apart from each other is that the substance gets bigger – it expands. This is most obvious along the longest side of an object.

Comment

The question asks you to use the particle model in your explanation. So describe what happens to the particles when the substance is heated. Then make sure that you relate this to how that expansion shows itself in the substance as a whole – describe some evidence of the substance getting bigger.

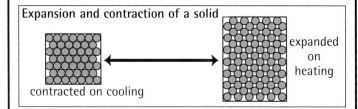

Expansion and contraction of a solid

contracted on cooling — expanded on heating

Now try these!

Gravy powder contains:
- a brown substance to make the gravy brown
- cornflour to make the gravy thick.

Dan mixed some gravy powder with cold water in a beaker. An hour later, the contents of the beaker looked like this:

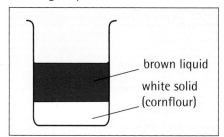

brown liquid
white solid (cornflour)

1 Use these words to fill the gaps in the sentences:

   solvent solution soluble insoluble

   a The brown substance dissolves in water to form a brown _____ .

   b The cornflour settles at the bottom of the beaker because it is _____ in water.

   c Water is the _____ in this experiment. *(3 marks)*

2 Dan wanted to separate the brown liquid from the white solid. What could he do to separate them? *(1 mark)*

3 Dan put a little of the brown liquid in a dish. The next day there was only a brown solid left in the dish. What had happened to the water? *(1 mark)*

Geological changes

1 *Water is the only substance that does not contract when it freezes.*

- As it cools from 4 °C to 0 °C, **water expands**. This explains why ice floats in water.

- The forces that are exerted when water in a crack of a rock freezes can be enough to break large rocks into smaller ones. When the freezing of water breaks down rocks, **weathering** is taking place.

- Once inside the crack, the water will expand as it freezes if the temperature falls to 0 °C. As it expands, the water exerts a force on the rock large enough to push it apart. If this happens again and again, pieces will be broken away from the rock.

Weathering of rocks

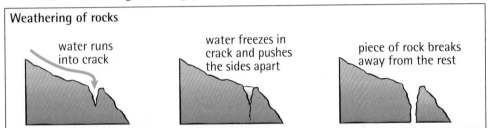

water runs into crack

water freezes in crack and pushes the sides apart

piece of rock breaks away from the rest

2 *Continual expansion and contraction due to changes in the temperature of the surroundings can also cause weathering of rocks.*

Rocks in the desert get very hot during the day and very cold at night. Over long periods the expansion during the day and the contraction during the night create forces within the rocks which cause them to break up.

3 *There are three different groups of rocks: sedimentary, metamorphic and igneous.*

The **formation process is different** for the three types of rock. Each type of rock is different because of the way it was formed.

Each rock type contains **different minerals** and has a **different texture**, due to their different processes of formation.

rock type	formation	appearance	examples
sedimentary	Sediments fall to the bottom of the sea and are compressed together by the weight of the sediments above.	Layered and often contain fossils.	limestone sandstone
igneous	When molten rock (magma) from inside the Earth cools.	Interlocking crystals of different sizes. No layers can be seen.	granite basalt
metamorphic	Existing rocks which are changed by high temperatures or high pressures.	Crystalline with streaks or layers of different types.	marble slate

4 *The recycling of all existing rocks to form new rocks takes millions of years. This is summarised in the rock cycle.*

The rock cycle

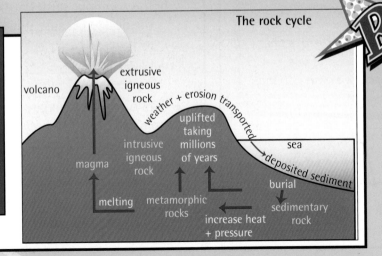

volcano

extrusive igneous rock

weather + erosion transported

uplifted taking millions of years

intrusive igneous rock

magma

sea

deposited sediment

melting

metamorphic rocks

increase heat + pressure

burial

sedimentary rock

Remember

The three different types of rock are formed in different ways and this is responsible for the physical and chemical differences between them.

Copy and complete

rock type	appearance	example
metamorphic rocks		granite
sedimentary rocks	interlocking crystals and no layers	limestone
	streaks and layers of different types	

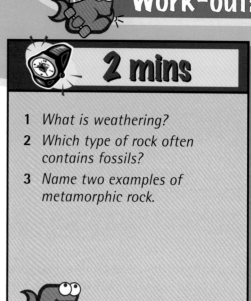

1 What is weathering?
2 Which type of rock often contains fossils?
3 Name two examples of metamorphic rock.

Question and model answer

Granite and basalt are igneous rocks made up of crystals, but do not contain any fossils.

Explain how igneous rocks are formed and why they do not contain fossils.

Igneous rocks are formed when molten rock (magma) from within the Earth cools and becomes a crystalline solid. They do not contain fossils because they were formed in conditions deep underground where living things do not exist.

Comment

Make sure that you answer both parts of the question. The second part follows from the first because igneous rocks are solidified magma, which has come from within the Earth. To say that the fossils are destroyed by the high temperatures in the magma would be incorrect because the living things were never there in the first place so could not be destroyed by the heat.

Now try these!

The action of weather and plants on rocks or building materials is weathering. The material is damaged but nothing gets taken away. When material is broken down and removed from the area the process is called erosion.

1 For the examples described in the table, tick **one** box in each row to show if the example is **weathering**, **erosion** or **neither**. *(4 marks)*

example	weathering	erosion	neither
The stones in an old wall have been pushed apart by the roots of weeds.			
An old granite gravestone is still smooth and shiny.			
A clay flower pot in the garden has crumbled and broken into pieces during the winter.			
Some soil has been washed from a flower bed by rain.			

2 How does water cause weathering of a brick? *(1 mark)*

Chemical reactions

1 There are many different types of chemical reaction: such as *oxidation, combustion, thermal decomposition, displacement, neutralisation* and *reduction reactions.*

Oxidation reactions: these are reactions where **oxygen is gained** by one of the reactants. Aluminium reacts with oxygen in the air to form aluminium oxide:

> aluminium + oxygen ⟶ aluminium oxide

Combustion reactions: these are oxidation reactions that **release large quantities of thermal energy.** When a fuel burns it produces water and carbon dioxide with the release of energy:

> fuel + oxygen ⟶ (*energy released*) water + carbon dioxide

Thermal decomposition reactions: these are reactions where substances **decompose when they are heated.** Calcium carbonate decomposes to form calcium oxide and carbon dioxide when it is heated:

> calcium carbonate ⟶ calcium oxide + carbon dioxide

Displacement reactions: these are reactions where **one metal displaces another metal from a compound.** Here, magnesium displaces copper:

> magnesium + copper sulphate ⟶ magnesium sulphate + copper

Neutralisation reactions: these are reactions where an **acid reacts with an alkali to form a metal salt and water.** Hydrochloric acid and sodium hydroxide are neutralised and form sodium chloride and water:

> hydrochloric acid + sodium hydroxide ⟶ sodium chloride + water

Reduction reactions: these reactions allow **metals to be produced from metal oxides.** Iron oxide can be dug from the ground. In a **blast furnace,** the iron oxide reacts with carbon monoxide to produce iron and carbon dioxide:

> iron oxide + carbon monoxide ⟶ iron + carbon dioxide

The iron has lost the oxygen with which it was combined. The iron has been reduced. This reaction, reduction, is the opposite of oxidation and can be used to separate most metals from their oxides.

2 In some chemical reactions the products aren't useful.

- The corrosion of iron and steel is called **rusting.** Iron reacts with water and oxygen in the air to form **iron oxide.** This reduces the strength of the iron and it either has to be protected to prevent rusting (by painting or coating with another metal) or replaced.

- Some foods spoil when the **chemicals they contain are oxidised** by oxygen in the air. Milk turns sour because the fats and oils that it contains are oxidised to compounds that have an unpleasant smell.

3 Combustion reactions produce *thermal energy.*

Controlled burning of fossil fuels in power stations drives generators that **produce electricity.**

Electricity is a very convenient and usable energy resource but it has adverse effects on the environment:

- it **increases the concentration of carbon dioxide** in the atmosphere, which may **increase global warming**
- it **produces pollutants,** such as **sulphur dioxide,** that react with water in the atmosphere and this falls as **acid rain.**

Not all chemical reactions are helpful.

Work-out!

Copy and complete

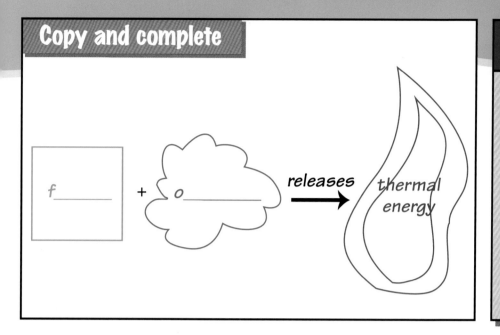

f_____ + o_____ → releases → thermal energy

2 mins

1 What sort of reaction allows metals to be produced from their oxides?
2 What is the corrosion of iron and steel called?
3 Which pollutant reacts with water in the atmosphere and falls as acid rain?

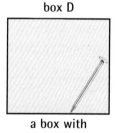

Question and model answer

Why are chemical reactions useful?

Chemical reactions are useful because we use them to produce a wide range of useful products. They are used to produce the chemicals used to make plastics, drugs used as medicines, cement used to construct buildings, cosmetics and household cleaners.

Comment

Virtually all materials, including those in living systems, are made as a result of chemical reactions. Respiration and photosynthesis are examples in living things. Although the answer refers to chemical reactions producing chemicals in industry, there are many chemical reactions which take place all around us every day. Cooking our food and using superglue are two examples.

Now try these!

Four shiny iron nails are put in small sealed plastic boxes. The labels show what else is in the boxes.

box A — drying agent — a box with dry air in it

box B — water — a box with damp air in it

box C — concentrated hydrocholoric acid — a box with damp, acidic air in it

box D — a box with no air in it

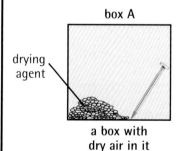
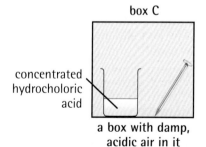

1a In which **two** boxes will the iron not rust or corrode? *(2 marks)*

b In which box will the iron corrode most? *(1 mark)*

2 Many parts of bicycles are made from iron or steel. These parts can rust easily, even indoors.

Give **two** ways to stop these parts rusting. *(2 marks)*

Word equations

1 A word equation gives a simple summary of a chemical reaction between two or more substances.

- A word equation only **contains the names of the substances** that are involved in the reaction.

- The substances that react together are called the **reactants**.

- In chemical reactions the reactants are changed into new substances, called **products**. During these reactions the **total mass of the reactants is always equal to the total mass of the products.**

2 Every chemical reaction can be represented by a word equation.

- Word equations use the names of the chemicals involved in the reaction and show which substances react to form which products.

- Word equations must be written in a very specific way.

- On the left-hand side you write the names of the substances that you start with – **the reactants**.

- On the right-hand side you write the names of the substances left at the end of the reaction – **the products**.

- The general form of a word equation is:

reactant + reactant $\longrightarrow$ product + product

3 An example for the reaction between calcium and water is:
calcium + water $\longrightarrow$ calcium hydroxide + hydrogen

- When calcium is added to water, the reaction produces calcium hydroxide and hydrogen.

- Calcium and water are the reactants.

- Calcium hydroxide and hydrogen are the products.

- The arrow points from the reactants to the products.

- The '+' sign means 'and'.

- This word equation should be read as:

  'Calcium and water react to produce calcium hydroxide and hydrogen.'

4 A word equation only summarises the names of the substance that takes part in the reaction and its products.

A word equation **does not** provide information about:

- the **quantities** of either the reactants or products

- the **physical states** of the reactants and products (whether solid, liquid or gas)

- the **rate of the reaction**

- any **special conditions** necessary for the reaction to take place.

A word equation tells you which substances take part in a chemical reaction and the names of the products of the reaction.

Copy and complete

Word equations tell you about . . .	Word equations do not tell you about . . .
reactants	_____
_____	reaction rates
	_____
	special conditions

1 What is the general name for the substances that take part in a chemical reaction?
2 Which substances are written on the right-hand side of a word equation?
3 What is important about the total mass of substances both before the reaction starts and once it has ended?

Question and model answer

An iron nail is put into some blue copper sulphate solution. A reaction takes place between the iron and the copper sulphate.

Write a word equation to summarise this reaction:

iron + copper sulphate ⟶ iron sulphate + copper

Comments

A word equation must be written in the form described opposite. You must use the + sign between the reactants and between the products, joining the two sides with the ⟶ sign.

The question tells you that the reactants are iron and copper sulphate.

A displacement reaction takes place in which the iron displaces the copper from the copper sulphate. The iron combines with the sulphate to become iron sulphate and the copper metal is left uncombined.

Now try these!

Kerry made some copper sulphate crystals. She wrote a description of what she did:

I heated some dilute sulphuric acid in a beaker and added some copper oxide to it. I stirred the mixture until it became a clear blue colour. I added more copper oxide until no more would react and then filtered the mixture into a dish. A black solid was left on the filter paper. I left the solution in the dish for a week and saw that the liquid had gone and blue crystals were left.

Use the information in Kerry's description to answer the questions below.

1 What colour is:
   a copper sulphate solution? *(1 mark)*
   b copper oxide? *(1 mark)*

2 Write down a word equation for the reaction which took place in the beaker. *(1 mark)*

_____ + _____ ⟶ _____ + water

3 Why did Kerry have to filter the mixture? *(1 mark)*

Metals and non-metals

1 Elements are divided into two groups: metals and non-metals.

- The **physical properties** of elements can be used to classify them as either **metallic** or **non-metallic**.

- Metals have many properties in common, but non-metals are much more varied in their properties. There are some notable exceptions in each group, which have some of the properties of that group but not others.
  For example, **mercury** is a metal but it is a liquid at room temperature. **Carbon** is a non-metal but in one form, diamond, is very strong and another form, graphite, is a good conductor of electricity.

2 Here are some examples of common metals and non-metals:

metals		non-metals	
name	symbol	name	symbol
iron	Fe	carbon	C
copper	Cu	sulphur	S
magnesium	Mg	oxygen	O
aluminium	Al	chlorine	Cl
chromium	Cr	bromine	Br

3 Metals take part in many important chemical reactions.

The reactions between metals and oxygen, water and acids can be summarised by these equations.

general	example	symbol
metal + oxygen ⟶ metal oxide	magnesium + oxygen ⟶ magnesium oxide	$2Mg + O_2 \longrightarrow 2MgO$
metal + water ⟶ metal hydroxide + hydrogen	sodium + water ⟶ sodium hydroxide + hydrogen	$2K + 2H_2O \longrightarrow 2KOH + H_2$
metal + acid ⟶ metal salt + hydrogen	zinc + hydrochloric acid ⟶ zinc chloride + hydrogen	$Zn + 2HCl \longrightarrow ZnCl_2 + H_2$

4 Metals and non-metals have some general properties that you will need to know.

metals	non-metals
usually silvery	different colours
good electrical conductors	poor electrical conductors
good thermal conductors	poor thermal conductors
usually strong	usually weak
flexible	brittle

metals	non-metals
shiny	dull
usually have a high melting point	usually have a low melting point
mostly solids at room temperature	solid, liquid or gas at room temperature
some are magnetic	none are magnetic

Metals and non-metals have different physical properties.

Copy and complete

metals	non-metals
_____	different colours
electrical conductors	_____
_____	weak
flexible	_____
_____	dull

1 *Which elements do the symbols Mg, Cu and Cl represent?*
2 *Which metallic element is a liquid at room temperature?*
3 *What are the products of a reaction between a metal and an acid?*

Question and model answer

What properties of iron make it suitable for making saucepans?

Iron:

- is strong
- is a good thermal conductor
- has a high melting point.

Comments

Your answer to this question must list only those particular physical properties that make iron a suitable material for saucepans.

A saucepan must be a strong container, which allows thermal energy to pass through it so that its contents become hot quickly. It must also not melt when it is being heated – so its melting point must be above 100°C.

Now try these!

Gold, iron and magnesium are elements that conduct electricity. Sulphur and phosphorous are elements that do not conduct electricity.

When iron and sulphur are heated together, they react to form a new substance called iron sulphide.

1 From the substances named above, give:
  a the name of a metal *(1 mark)*
  b the name of an element that is a non-metal *(1 mark)*
  c the name of an element that will rust *(1 mark)*
  d the name of a compound *(1 mark)*

2 When magnesium and sulphur are heated together, they react. Write the name of the compound that is formed when magnesium reacts with sulphur. *(1 mark)*

The reactivity series

1 Some metals are more reactive than others.

- The speed and violence of the reactions of metals with oxygen, water and acids are different for different metals.

- Some metals react very rapidly and others do not react at all. This is because some metals are more reactive than others.

3 The metals follow the same order of reactivity in all of their reactions.

It is possible, because of this, to make predictions about the reactions of metals with other substances. By using differences in reactivity it is possible to predict, for example, that:

- zinc will displace lead from lead nitrate

- calcium will displace magnesium from magnesium sulphate.

These are only predictions based on the knowledge of the reactivity series. They do not tell us anything about the actual reactions that may take place.

The reactivity series lists metals in order of their reactivity, the most reactive at one end and the least reactive at the other.

2 The reactivity series of metals can be established by using the results of a series of displacement reactions.

- A displacement reaction takes place when a **more reactive metal reacts with a compound of a less reactive metal**.

- If a metal A is placed into a solution of a salt (compound) of metal B, a reaction will take place if A is more reactive than B – A will replace B in the salt. If A is less reactive than B, no reaction will take place.
  For example, when a piece of **iron** is placed in a solution of **copper sulphate**, it becomes covered with a thin layer of copper. This can be summarised by this word equation:

> iron + copper sulphate ⟶ iron sulphate + copper

The copper has been replaced by iron in the compound. Iron must be more reactive than copper so is higher in the reactivity series.

The reactivity series

metal	symbol
potassium	K
sodium	Na
calcium	Ca
magnesium	Mg
aluminium	Al
carbon	C
zinc	Zn
iron	Fe
tin	Sn
lead	Pb
hydrogen	H
copper	Cu
silver	Ag
gold	Au

most reactive

The non-metals carbon and hydrogen are included because they both react with some metals but not with others.

least reactive

Copy and complete

metal	symbol	
potassium	_____	most reactive
_____	Na	
calcium	_____	
_____	Mg	
aluminium	_____	
_____	C	
zinc	_____	
_____	Fe	
tin	_____	
_____	Pb	
hydrogen	_____	
_____	Cu	
silver	_____	
_____	Au	least reactive

2 mins

1 *What is a displacement reaction?*
2 *Which of these metals is the most reactive: lead, calcium or aluminium?*
3 *What is the reactivity series?*

Now try these!

1 Copper reacts with silver nitrate solution.

   a Complete the word equation for the reaction:

   copper + silver nitrate ⟶

   _____ + _____ *(2 marks)*

   b Platinum does **not** react with silver nitrate. Put the metals platinum, copper and silver in the correct order according to their reactivity. *(1 mark)*

   most reactive _____

   _____

   least reactive _____

2 In many houses the hot water pipes are made from copper and the boiler is made from iron. Which of these metals will corrode first? Explain your answer. *(1 mark)*

Question and model answer

What prediction could you make about what happens when copper is placed in a solution of lead nitrate?

You would predict that no reaction would occur.

Comments

A prediction about what will happen in this particular reaction has to be based on your knowledge of similar reactions and the relative reactivity of copper and lead.

Copper is lower in the reactivity series than lead. Because of this copper is unable to displace lead from the lead nitrate solution – so no reaction will take place.

Acids and alkalis

 Substances are acids, alkalis or neutral.

- Vinegar, oranges and grapefruit juice all contain acids. **Hydrochloric acid** and **sulphuric acid** are used in science lessons.
- All acids contain the element **hydrogen** and react in the same ways with substances, such as metals and alkalis.
- Alkalis are the **solutions of bases** (metal oxides).
- Many soaps, oven cleaners and washing powders contain alkalis. Solutions of sodium hydroxide and calcium hydroxide are examples of alkalis that you may have come across in your science lessons.
- Liquids and solutions that are neither acidic nor alkaline are neutral. Water is an example of a neutral liquid.

Indicators can be used to classify liquids or solutions as acidic, neutral or alkaline.

- A common indicator is **litmus**. Litmus remains unchanged in a neutral solution, turns **red in an acidic solution** and turns **blue in an alkaline solution**.
- **Universal indicator** can measure the acidity or alkalinity of a solution. It is a mixture of several dyes extracted from plants. The overall colour of the indicator solution is compared with the range of colours in the pH scale to give a measure of acidity or alkalinity.
- A **neutral** solution has a **pH of 7**. A solution with a pH less than 7 is **acidic**, with the strongest acids having the lowest pH value. A solution with a pH greater than 7 is **alkaline**, with the strongest alkalis having the highest pH value.

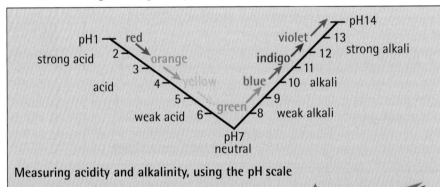

Measuring acidity and alkalinity, using the pH scale

 Acids take part in some important chemical reactions.

- The reactions between acids and metals are all very similar and can be summarised in this word equation:

  metal + acid ⟶ metal salt + hydrogen

For example:

  magnesium + sulphuric acid ⟶ magnesium sulphate + hydrogen

- The reaction of acids and metal carbonates can be summarised in this word equation:

  acid + metal carbonate ⟶ metal salt + carbon dioxide + water

For example:

  sulphuric acid + sodium carbonate ⟶ sodium sulphate + carbon dioxide + water

- The reaction of acids with alkalis can be summarised in this word equation:

  acid + alkali ⟶ metal salt + water

For example:

  sulphuric acid + potassium hydroxide ⟶ potassium sulphate + water

Remember

Universal indicator is used to show the strength of acids and alkalis.
A neutral solution has pH7. Acids have pH values less than 7. Alkalis have pH values greater than 7.

Copy and complete

	acid	neutral	alkali
pH values	_____	7	8–14
colour of UI	red to yellow	___	blue to violet
common substances	vinegar grapefruit juice	water	_____

2 mins

1 Which element is contained in all acids?
2 What colour is litmus in an alkaline solution?
3 What are the products of the reactions between acids and alkalis?

Questions and model answers

Different plants grow well in different soil pHs. Some plants grow well in neutral soils. Heather grows best in acidic soil. Cabbage grows better in alkaline soil.

1 What is the pH of a neutral soil?
Neutral soil is pH7.

2 What is the pH of the moorland soil where heather grows well?
Moorland soil has a pH less than 7.

3 What is the pH of the garden soil where cabbage grows well?
The garden soil would have a pH greater than 7.

Comments

There is a great deal of information in this question. Take your time to read it carefully and make the connection between the named plants and the pH of the soil where they grow well.

The chemicals in the soil in different places determine its pH. Universal indicator solution can be used to test the pH of soil samples.

Acidic soils have a pH less than 7. Alkaline soils have a pH greater than 7.

Now try these!

Bees and wasps are both insects that use a sting as part of their defence. The pH values of their stings are shown on the diagrams.

1 Complete the table below to show whether the stings are acidic or alkaline and what colour they would turn universal indicator paper. (2 marks)

bee

bee sting, pH2

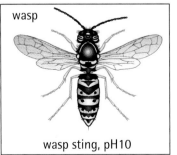

wasp

wasp sting, pH10

	acidic or alkaline	colour of universal indicator paper
bee sting (pH2)		
wasp sting (pH10)		

2 The table below shows five household substances and the pH of each substance.

name of substance	pH of substance
bicarbonate toothpaste	8
lemon juice	3
vinegar	4
washing soda	11
water	7

Give the name of **one** substance in the table that would neutralise each sting:

a bee sting (1 mark)
b wasp sting. (1 mark)

Neutralisation

1 Reactions between acids and alkalis are called neutralisation reactions.

- Neutralisation reactions occur when an **acid reacts with an alkali to produce a metal salt and water**. These can be summarised by the general word equation:

  acid + alkali ⟶ salt + water

- Hydrochloric acid and sodium hydroxide neutralise each other to form sodium chloride and water.

  hydrochloric acid + sodium hydroxide ⟶ sodium chloride + water

- Sulphuric acid and potassium hydroxide neutralise each other to form potassium sulphate and water.

  sulphuric acid + potassium hydroxide ⟶ potassium sulphate + water

- The resulting solution in both of these reactions is neutral: pH7.

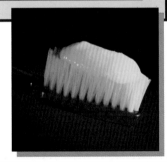

2 The process of neutralisation can be used in many ways.

- **Excess stomach acid** can cause the pain we call indigestion. Cures for indigestion are called antacids and are weak alkalis. By taking some magnesium hydroxide in water, excess stomach acid can be neutralised.

- **Farmers add lime** (calcium hydroxide) to soil to neutralise excess acidity which might otherwise prevent their crops from growing.

- The acids that build up on our **teeth** can be neutralised by brushing them with toothpaste, which contains an alkali.

3 Acids can also have some adverse effects on our environment.

Sulphur dioxide and **nitrogen dioxide** are produced by power stations and some factories. In the air these gases react with water to form weak solutions of **sulphuric acid** and **nitric acid**. This solution might eventually fall as **acid rain** and have the following effects:
- the corrosion of metals exposed to the air
- the chemical weathering of rocks
- washing nutrient salts out of top soil
- increasing the acidity of rivers and lakes
- killing foliage of plants (see photo).

Alkalis can be used to neutralise soil acidity, excess stomach acid and the acids that build up on our teeth.

Copy and complete

Neutralisation

☐ + alkali ⟶ ☐ + water

Question and model answer

Explain how applying baking soda to a bee sting and vinegar to a wasp sting can reduce the effects of the stings.

A bee sting contains an acid. By applying baking soda, an alkali, the effect of the sting can be neutralised.

A wasp sting contains an alkali. By applying vinegar, an acid, the effect of the sting can be neutralised.

Comment

To get full credit for your answer when you are asked to 'explain' something you must provide the reason. It would not have been good enough to just write that the bee sting is acidic and the baking soda is alkaline. The reason why the effects of the sting are reduced is because of the neutralisation reaction that takes place.

Now try these!

Sodium hydrogencarbonate is present in indigestion powders. It is often called bicarbonate of soda. Sodium hydrogencarbonate:

- is a white solid
- forms a solution with a pH of about 8.5
- does not smell
- is not poisonous.

1a Is sodium hyrogencarbonate solution acidic, alkaline or neutral? *(1 mark)*

b Indigestion can be caused by too much acid in the stomach. Which **two** pieces of information in the list are the most important reasons why sodium hydrogencarbonate can be used as an indigestion powder? *(2 marks)*

2 Nitric acid reacts with sodium hydrogencarbonate. The salt formed is a nitrate. Fill in the boxes to complete the word equation. *(1 mark)*

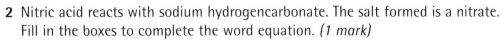

sodium hydrogencarbonate + ☐ ⟶ carbon dioxide + water + ☐

3 An indigestion powder contains sodium hydrogencarbonate and a small amount of citric acid. The powder starts to fizz when it is added to water. What gas is given off when the mixture fizzes? *(1 mark)*

Electrical charge

- The friction between the two materials causes **electrons to be removed** from one of them and added to the other.
- When a material **gains electrons**, it becomes **positively charged**.
- The material that **loses the electrons** becomes **negatively charged**.
- These charges remain at the point they are produced if the material is an **insulator**.

2 Charged objects interact with each other.

- The forces that charges exert on each other cause these interactions.
- Objects with **similar charges repel** each other.
- Objects with **opposite charges attract** each other.

3 Here is how charges interact. Remember – like charges repel, unlike charges attract.

	positive ⊕	negative ⊖
positive ⊕	repel each other	attract each other
negative ⊖	attract each other	repel each other

4 Charges can *move through some materials*.

- If the material on which the charges are produced is a **conductor**, the charges will **flow away** from the point where they were produced.
- This is because they can move freely though materials like metals, which are good conductors.
- The flow of charged particles through a conductor is called an **electrical current**.

5 The electrical current that flows around an electric circuit is a *flow of charged particles*.

- The charges **transfer energy** from a battery or other power supply to the components in the circuit.
- Electrical current is the **flow of negatively charged particles** called electrons around an electrical circuit.
- The current is measured in **amperes** (symbol, A) using an ammeter.
- The current that leaves a component, such as a lamp or a motor, is the same as the current that enters the component.
- Electrical current is not 'used up' by components in an electric circuit.

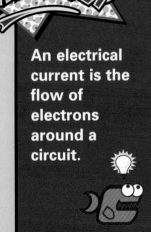

Remember

An electrical current is the flow of electrons around a circuit.

Copy and complete

_____ charges
repel each other.

Opposite charges
_____ each other.

1 *How do similar charges interact with each other?*
2 *What happens to electrical charges produced on a conducting material?*
3 *What is the measurement unit of electrical current?*

Question and model answer

Explain why you can sometimes see small sparks when you take a jumper off in a darkened room as well as hear a 'crackling' noise.

As you pull the jumper over your head, the friction between your head and the jumper produces charges on both you and the jumper. These charges are attracted to each other and discharge each other by jumping across small air gaps – creating a small electric current. The spark is visible briefly as this happens, as well as producing the crackling noise.

Comments

An explanation requires the reason for the answer not just the answer itself.

It is sometimes helpful to write your answer as a description in the order the events happen. This makes it clear what causes things to happen. In this case, the charges have to be produced before they can be discharged and produce the sparks and crackles.

Now try these!

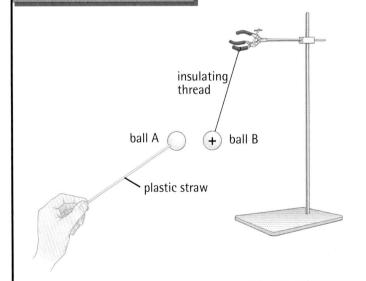

insulating thread

ball A

(+) ball B

plastic straw

Two polystyrene balls, A and B, are shown below. Both balls are charged. Ball B is positively charged. The diagram shows what happens when ball A is brought near ball B.

1 Ball **A** is charged. Describe one method by which ball **A** could have been charged. *(1 mark)*

2 Is ball **A** positively or negatively charged? Explain your answer. *(1 mark)*

3 Ball **A** is moved a little closer to ball **B**. Which way does ball **B** move? *(1 mark)*

Electrical circuits

1 **The first type of electrical circuit you need to learn about is *series* circuits.**

- There is only **one current path** between the two terminals of the power supply.
- A **switch** placed anywhere in the circuit will **affect all of the components** in the circuit.
- The **current is the same at all points in the circuit** – the reading on an ammeter, connected anywhere in the circuit, will be the same.

- The **size of the current** that passes in the circuit **depends on the number of cells** in the battery (or the voltage of the power supply) and the **number and type of components** in the circuit.
- **Increasing the number of cells** in the circuit (or the voltage of the power supply) will **increase the current**, but **adding more components** (bulbs, motors or buzzers) will **reduce the current** because there is more resistance in the circuit.

A series circuit
The switch turns on or off all of the components in the circuit.
The current is the same at every point in the circuit.

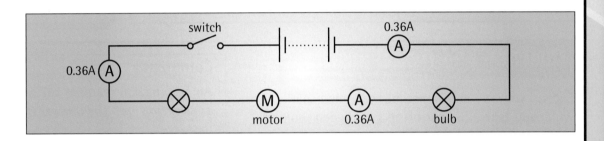

2 **The second type of electrical circuit you need to learn about is *parallel* circuits.**

- There is **more than one current path** between the terminals of the power supply.
- A **switch** in a parallel circuit will only affect those components in the **same current path**.

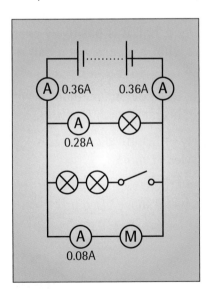

A parallel circuit
The switch turns on or off only the two bulbs in the central branch of the circuit. The current is different in different parts of the circuit.

- The current splits and rejoins at the circuit junctions. At each junction the total current entering is the same as the total current leaving.
- The **current is not the same in all parts of the circuit.** The current in each branch of the circuit will depend on the components in that branch. The current in each branch of the circuit can only be measured by connecting an ammeter into that branch.
- The **total of the currents in the branches** of the circuit is the same as the current between the power supply and a junction.

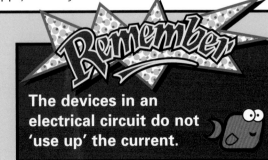

The devices in an electrical circuit do not 'use up' the current.

Copy and complete

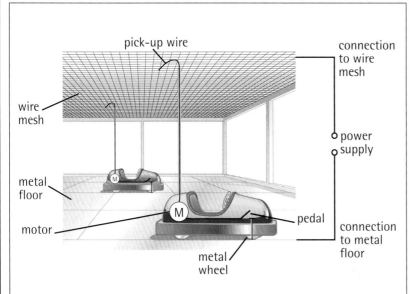

s _____
circuit

p _____
circuit

Question and model answer

What is an electric current and how is it measured?

Electric current is a flow of charged particles (electrons) around an electric circuit. The charges transfer energy from the power supply to the components in the circuit.

Electric current is measured in amperes (A) using an ammeter, which is connected into the circuit in series with the other components.

Comment

There are two parts to this question. Firstly you are asked to define an electric current - explain what it is. Then you are asked to explain how is it measured. Make sure that you provide an answer to both parts.

Now try these!

The diagram shows two dodgem cars at a fairground. The circuit symbols for the motor and pedal for each dodgem car are shown on the diagram.

pick-up wire

connection to wire mesh

wire mesh

power supply

metal floor

motor

pedal

connection to metal floor

metal wheel

1 Complete the following sentence.

Each dodgem car is connected to the power supply through the _____ , which is in contact with the wire mesh, and through the _____ , which is in contact with the metal floor. *(1 mark)*

2 Even when the power supply is switched on, the dodgem car will **not** move until the pedal is pressed.
Give the reason for this. *(1 mark)*

3 A man looks after the dodgem cars during the rides. Why does the man **not** get an electric shock as he walks across the metal floor? *(1 mark)*

1 *The most common magnetic materials are iron, steel and nickel.*

- When a piece of one of these materials is magnetised we call it a **magnet**.

- Every magnet has a space around it where it **exerts a force** on other magnets or pieces of magnetic material. This is called its **magnetic field**.

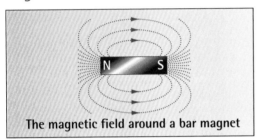

The magnetic field around a bar magnet

- All magnets have **two poles**: a north pole and a south pole. These are the parts where the **magnetic force is strongest**.

- Magnets exert forces on other magnets. **Opposite** magnetic poles (one north pole and one south pole) exert a **force of attraction** on each other. **Similar** magnetic poles (two north poles or two south poles) exert a **force of repulsion** on each other.

HELP! **Don't forget – like poles repel, and unlike poles attract.**

- Magnets always attract unmagnetised magnetic materials.

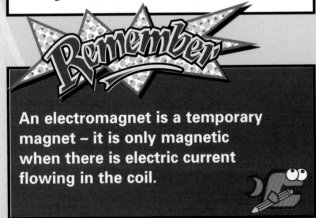

Remember

An electromagnet is a temporary magnet – it is only magnetic when there is electric current flowing in the coil.

2 *When an electric current flows through a wire, a very weak magnetic field is produced around the wire.*

- If the **wire is wound into a coil**, these very weak magnetic fields add together and look very similar to the field around a bar magnet.

- If an **iron bar** is placed through the middle of the coil, the magnetic field is concentrated into the bar and it behaves like a magnet. The only difference is that when the current is turned off the bar stops being magnetic.

- This is called an **electromagnet**. It is a temporary magnet, only being magnetised while the current is flowing in the coil.

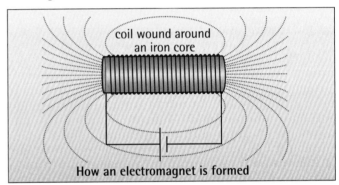

coil wound around an iron core

How an electromagnet is formed

3 *Electromagnets are used in a large number of appliances that we use every day.*

- They are used to make loudspeaker cones vibrate, in motors that turn lawnmower blades, and for recording onto audiotapes, videotapes and computer disks.

- A **relay** is a switch that uses an electromagnet. It is used in circuits where a small current or voltage is used to switch large currents or voltage on and off.

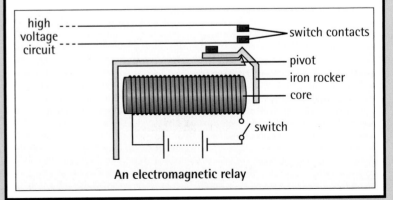

high voltage circuit — switch contacts — pivot — iron rocker — core — switch

An electromagnetic relay

Copy and complete

iron _____

+

_____ coil

+

electric_____

} electromagnet

1 What is the name for the space around a magnet or electromagnet where they exert a force on other magnets or pieces of magnetic material?
2 What is the effect of placing an iron bar through the middle of a coil of wire carrying an electric current?
3 What is an electrical relay?

Question and model answer

Complete this paragraph by inserting the correct words in the spaces.

When a current passes through a coil of wire a **1** _____ magnetic **2** _____ is produced in the space around the coil. This can be concentrated by placing an **3** _____ bar through the centre of the coil. The bar will then behave like a **4** _____. When the current is turned off the bar will **5** _____ being magnetic. An electromagnet only behaves like a magnet when the **6** _____ is flowing in the coil.

1 temporary   2 field   3 iron
4 magnet   5 stop   6 current

Comment

Read each sentence in full before deciding which word to put in each space. Also look for the clues in the text. The word 'an' in front of number 3 means that the word that goes in that space must begin with a vowel.

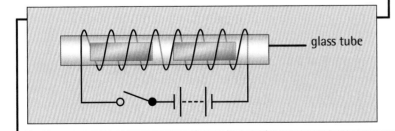

Now try these!

A pupil wound a coil of copper wire around a glass tube and connected the wire to a battery. She placed a compass at each end of the tube and one compass beside the tube, as shown.

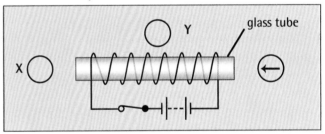

1a Complete the diagram by drawing arrows in compasses X and Y to show the direction of the magnetic field. *(2 marks)*

b Draw an arrow in the middle of the glass tube to show the direction of the magnetic field in the glass tube. *(1 mark)*

c When the switch is opened, in which direction will the three compass needles point? *(1 mark)*

2 Give **one** way to reverse the magnetic field around the glass tube. *(1 mark)*

3a Two pieces of iron are placed inside the glass tube (see diagram, left). When the switch is closed, the magnetic field is the same as in the diagram above. The pieces of iron become magnetised. Label the four poles on the pieces of iron. *(1 mark)*

b When the switch was closed, the pieces of iron moved. Explain why they moved. *(1 mark)*

Speed

 1 The speed of a moving object is the measure of how quickly it moves from one place to another.

- This is often described as the **rate at which something is moving**.
- To work out the speed of a moving object you need two measurements – the **distance** the object travels and the **time** it takes to move that distance.
- Distance travelled is measured in metres (m).
- Time taken is measured in seconds (s).

 2 The speed of a moving object is calculated by dividing the distance travelled by the time taken.

This is summarised in this formula:

$$\text{speed} = \frac{\text{distance travelled}}{\text{time taken}}$$

The unit of speed is the metre per second (m/s)

$$\text{speed (m/s)} = \frac{\text{distance travelled (m)}}{\text{time taken (s)}}$$

 3 Speed can be measured in a range of different units.

The unit of speed depends on the units used to measure distance and time. The most common measures you will come across are:

- **miles per hour** (distance in miles, time in hours)
- **kilometres per hour** (distance in kilometres, time in hours).

 4 Here's an easy way to remember how to calculate speed.

$$\frac{d}{s \times t}$$

If **s**, **d** and **t** represent speed, distance and time, an easy way to remember this relationship is to use this triangle. Cover the one you want to find with your finger and it will show you how to calculate it.

 **Remember**

The speed of a moving object is the distance it travels divided by the time it takes to travel that distance.

Copy and complete

speed	=	distance	÷	_____
distance	=	_____	×	time
time	=	distance	_____	speed

2 mins

1 How is the speed of a moving object described?
2 What two quantities have to be measured in order to calculate speed?
3 What is the unit of speed used in science?

Question and model answer

object	distance travelled (m)	time taken (s)	speed (m/s)
passenger aeroplane	10 000	a	200
cycle	80	10	b
snail	0.5	100	c
sports car	d	3	40

Complete this table by calculating the values of a, b, c and d.

a 50 s　　**b** 8.0 m/s　　**c** 0.005 m/s　　**d** 120 m

Comments

Calculating speed uses the relationship of distance divided by time so b and c should not be difficult except that c is a very small number because snails move very slowly.

In order to get the correct answers to a and d it is important to be able to use the rearranged relationship.

Now try these!

1 A video recorder is loaded with a tape, which plays for 180 minutes. The length of the tape is 260 metres.

a Calculate the speed of the tape in metres per minute. *(1 mark)*

b What is the speed of the tape in metres per second? *(1 mark)*

2 To rewind the tape quickly, a different motor is used, which rewinds the tape at a maximum speed of 1.08 m/s.

a At this speed, how long would it take to rewind the tape completely? Give the units. *(1 mark)*

b In fact, it takes slightly longer than this to rewind the tape. Explain why. *(1 mark)*

Unbalanced forces

 If *balanced forces* act on an object they do not cause any changes.

- If an object remains in its present state of motion, either at rest (stationary) or moving in a straight line at a constant speed, the forces acting on it are **balanced**.

- If the forces are balanced, then each force is cancelled out by another force of **equal size** acting in the **opposite direction**.

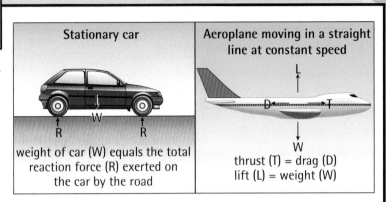

Stationary car

weight of car (W) equals the total reaction force (R) exerted on the car by the road

Aeroplane moving in a straight line at constant speed

thrust (T) = drag (D)
lift (L) = weight (W)

If the forces acting on an object are *unbalanced* then the *speed* of the object or the *direction* in which it is travelling will be changed.

- When an object either begins to move or increases its speed, the force in the direction of motion must be **greater than the force in the opposite direction**. The forces acting are then **unbalanced**.

- When an object slows down or is brought to a stop, the forces are also unbalanced but in this case the force opposing the motion is greater than the force in the direction of the motion.

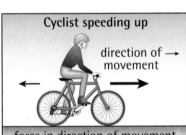

Cyclist speeding up

direction of → movement

force in direction of movement is greater than force in opposite direction

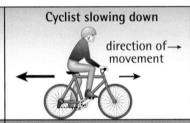

Cyclist slowing down

direction of → movement

force in direction of movement is smaller than force in opposite direction

---

 Friction is the force produced when two substances that are touching move past each other.

- In many cases this is useful. When we are walking friction is the force that stops our shoes from slipping. When we are driving, friction provides the necessary grip between the car tyres and the road.

- Friction also **resists the motion of objects** travelling through air, water or over rough surfaces.

- When an object moves through the air, it meets **air resistance**. This is the frictional force that opposes the motion of objects through the air. **The faster an object moves, the greater the air resistance force acting on it.**

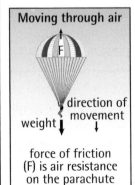

Moving through air

weight ↓

direction of movement ↓

force of friction (F) is air resistance on the parachute

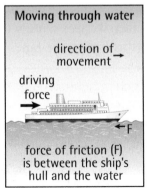

Moving through water

direction of movement →

driving force →

force of friction (F) is between the ship's hull and the water

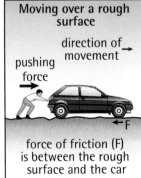

Moving over a rough surface

direction of movement →

pushing force →

force of friction (F) is between the rough surface and the car

Remember

A moving object will change its speed or direction of movement if the forces acting on it are unbalanced.

Copy and complete

Effect of forces on a moving object

forces	direction	speed
balanced	no change	_____
unbalanced	_____	may change

Question and model answer

What factors affect the distance travelled by a car in the time between the brakes being applied and the car coming to a halt?

The factors are:
- the mass of the car
- the speed of the car
- the force applied by the brakes
- the road conditions.

Comments

The question asks about factors, so there must be more than one – in this case there are four. You are only asked for the factors but it is helpful to know how they affect the stopping distance:
- The more massive a car; the greater the stopping distance.
- The faster a car is going; the greater the stopping distance.
- The more effective the brakes; the shorter the stopping distance.
- The less friction between the road and the tyres (when it is wet or icy); the greater the stopping distance.

Now try these!

The diagram shows a chain hanging down over the edge of a table.

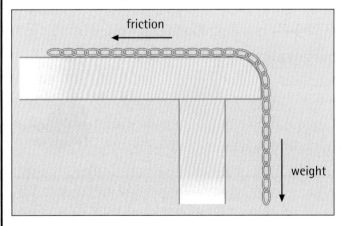

Two of the forces on the chain are:
- the weight of the part of the chain which is hanging over the edge
- friction between the chain and the table.

1 The chain is not moving. What does this tell you about the two forces acting on the chain? *(1 mark)*
2 The chain is moved slightly to the right. It begins to slide off the table.
   a What does this tell you about these two forces now? *(1 mark)*
   b Describe how the size of each of these forces changes as the chain slides off the table. *(2 marks)*
      i The weight of the part of the chain hanging over the edge
      ii The friction between the chain and the table.
   c How does the speed of the chain change as it slides off the table? *(1 mark)*

Turning forces

1 The point around which an object rotates is called the *pivot*.

- The **rotation** of an object is caused by the **application of a force**.
- The measure of **how effective the force is** at causing the rotation is called the **turning effect** or **moment** of the force.
- A moment is calculated by multiplying the size of the force in newtons (N) by the distance from the pivot in metres (m). This is summarised in the following formula:

  moment = force × distance from the pivot

- The unit of the moment is the newton metre (Nm).

2 The moment of a force can be increased by two factors.

- Increasing the size of the force will increase the moment of a force.
- Moving the point of application of the force further from the pivot will increase the moment of a force.
- The moment of the force (F) around the pivot (P) equals F × d. To increase the moment of the force, either increase the force (F) or use a longer pole.

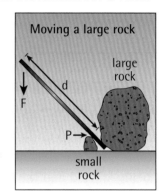

Moving a large rock

large rock

small rock

3 When an object resting on a pivot is not moving, it is described as balanced.

- The moments of the forces on either side of the pivot are equal even though the forces themselves may not be equal.
- The moment on the left of the pivot is called the **anticlockwise moment** because it is caused by a force that would turn the plank in that direction.

- The moment on the right is called the **clockwise moment**. It is caused by a force that would turn the plank in a clockwise direction.
- If there is more than one object exerting a force on either side of the pivot, the moment for each is calculated and added together to find the sum of the moments on that side.

A balanced beam

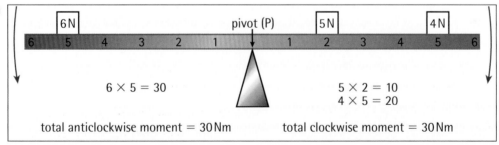

| 6N | | | | | pivot (P) | | 5N | | | 4N | |
| 6 | 5 | 4 | 3 | 2 | 1 | 1 | 2 | 3 | 4 | 5 | 6 |

6 × 5 = 30

5 × 2 = 10
4 × 5 = 20

total anticlockwise moment = 30 Nm

total clockwise moment = 30 Nm

Remember

The moment of the force (F) at a distance (d) from the pivot = F × d (Nm)

Work-out!

Copy and complete

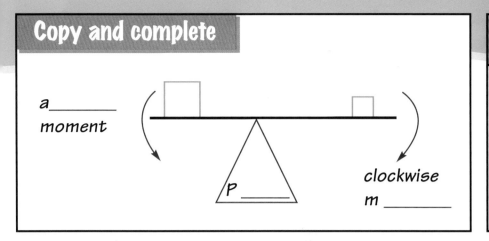

a_____ moment

P _____

clockwise
m _____

2 mins

1 *What is the name of the point around which an object rotates?*
2 *How can you increase the size of the moment of a force?*
3 *Which word is used to describe an object resting on a pivot and not moving?*

Question and model answer

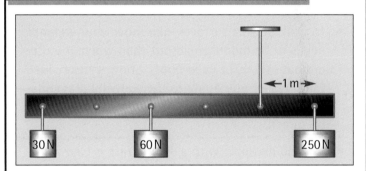

If this arm were set up, would it be balanced?

No, this arm would not be balanced – it would start to turn clockwise.

Comments

We can determine whether the arm will be balanced by calculating the moment due to each weight and them adding the moments on each side to find the total clockwise moment and the total anticlockwise moment. If these are the same the arm will be balanced.

total clockwise moment = 250 N × 1 m = 250 Nm

total anticlockwise moment:

60 N × 2 m = 120 Nm

30 N × 4 m = 120 Nm

total   = 240 Nm

The clockwise moment (250 Nm) is larger than the total anticlockwise moment (240 Nm) so the arm wouldn't balance and would start to turn clockwise.

Now try these!

A load of 5000 N is placed 8 m from the pivot.

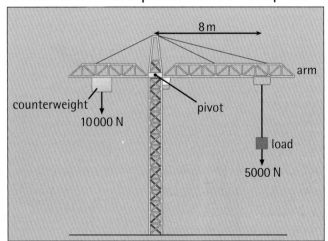

1 What is the turning moment of the load? Give the unit. *(2 marks)*
2 How far from the pivot must the 10 000 N counterweight be placed in order to balance the load? *(1 mark)*
3 The counterweight is placed 3 m from the pivot. What load could now be balanced 8 m from the pivot? *(1 mark)*

Pressure

 1 *The overall effect of a force on a surface is called pressure.*

- The pressure caused by a force depends on both the **size of the force** and the **size of the area** over which the force is exerted.
- The pressure on a surface is calculated by dividing the force measured in newtons (N) by the area measured in square metres (m²).

- This is summarised in the formula:

$$\text{pressure} = \frac{\text{force}}{\text{area}}$$

- The unit of pressure is the newton per square metre (N/m²).

 2 *The pressure on any surface can be changed.*

force	area	pressure
increase	keep constant	increases
keep constant	increase	decreases
decrease	keep constant	decreases
keep constant	decrease	increases

 4 *Here's an easy way to remember how to calculate pressure.*

If pressure, force and area are represented by **p**, **f** and **a**, an easy way to remember this relationship is to use this triangle. Cover the one you want to find with your finger and it will show you how to calculate it.

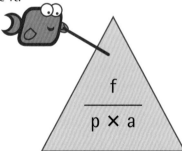

$$\text{pressure (N/m}^2) = \frac{\text{force (N)}}{\text{area (m}^2)}$$

 3 *Changing pressure can be helpful.*

- To walk on soft surfaces, like snow, your weight needs to be more spread out than when you use ordinary shoes or even boots. Snow shoes reduce the pressure you apply to the snow by providing a large area over which your weight (the force) can be spread.

- Cutting an apple with a sharp knife is easy because the force you exert is concentrated on a very small area, which means that the pressure you can apply is very high.

Low pressure

High pressure

Exerting a force on a small area will produce a high pressure. Spreading the force over a larger area will reduce the pressure.

Copy and complete

pressure = force ÷ _____

force = _____ × area

area = force ___ pressure

1 Which two quantities have to be measured in order to calculate pressure?
2 What is the unit of pressure?
3 How do snow shoes help us to walk on deep snow?

Question and model answer

What is the pressure applied to the ground by a box, which has a weight of 480 N, and which stands on a side, which has an area of 1.2 m²?

pressure = force/area

The pressure applied to the ground is:

$\frac{480}{1.2} = 400 \, N/m^2$

Comment

The weight of an object is its force due to gravity. Always write down the relationship you are using and show all of your working. Even if your final answer is incorrect you will get some marks for the working if it is correct. Do not forget to give the units of the quantity you have calculated – you may lose marks if you leave them out.

Now try these!

Karen wants to pump up her car tyre. Her pump has a piston with an area of 7 cm².

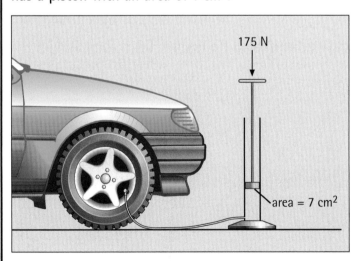

175 N

area = 7 cm²

Karen pushes the handle down with a force of 175 N.

1 What pressure does she exert on the air in the pump in N/cm²? *(1 mark)*

2 The air pressure in the tyre is 27 N/cm². What pressure would be needed **in the pump** in order to pump more air into the tyre? *(1 mark)*

3 Another of Karen's car tyres exerts a pressure of 30 N/cm² on the road. The area of the tyre in contact with the road is 95 cm². What is the force exerted by the tyre on the road, in N? *(1 mark)*

Reflection

Light travels much faster then sound.

- In air, **sound** travels at about **330 metres per second** (m/s). **Light** travels at **300 000 000 metres per second** (m/s), about one million times faster than sound!

- This is why events can be seen before sound from them can be heard.

- Another difference between light and sound is that because **light is a form of radiation** it can travel through space (a vacuum), whereas **sound travels as vibrations** of the particles of a medium (the solid, liquid or gas) through which it is passing.

Light travels in straight lines.

- This is why shadows are formed.

- If light could travel in curved lines or around corners then it would get behind opaque objects and shadows would not be formed.

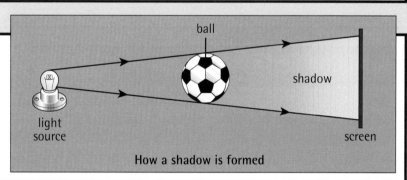

How a shadow is formed

Luminous objects can be seen because they produce their own light.

- All other objects are non-luminous.

- Almost all of these non-luminous objects reflect some of the light that falls on them. Most of these objects scatter light. That is, they reflect light in all directions.

- All objects can be seen because some of the light from them enters our eyes. Mirrors, however, reflect light in a regular and predictable way because of their surface and shape.

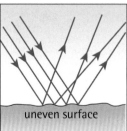

uneven surface

Scattering from an uneven surface

plane surface

Direct reflection from a plane surface

Plane mirrors reflect light from their surface at the same angle as the light strikes the surface.

- This can be summarised by:

  the angle of incidence (i) = the angle of reflection (r)

- The ray of light striking the mirror is called the **incident ray**.

- The ray of light leaving the mirror is called the **reflected ray**.

- The dashed line is called the **normal**. This is a line at right angles to the surface of the mirror where the light strikes the mirror.

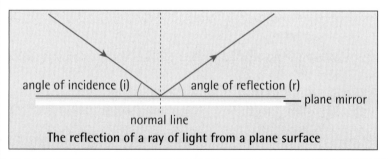

angle of incidence (i)　　angle of reflection (r)
plane mirror
normal line
The reflection of a ray of light from a plane surface

Light travels in straight lines and we see objects because light reflected from them enters our eyes.

Copy and complete

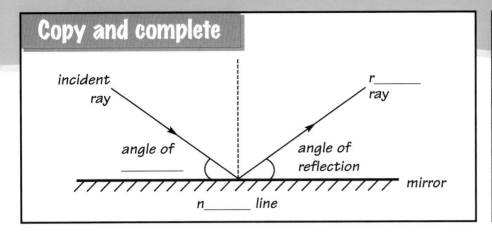

incident ray

r_____ ray

angle of _____

angle of reflection

mirror

n_____ line

2 mins

1 At what speed does light travel?
2 What is a luminous object?
3 What is the name of a line drawn at right angles to the surface of a plane mirror?

Question and model answer

A simple periscope can be used to see over the heads of a crowd attending a public event. Draw a diagram of the arrangement of mirrors in a simple periscope.

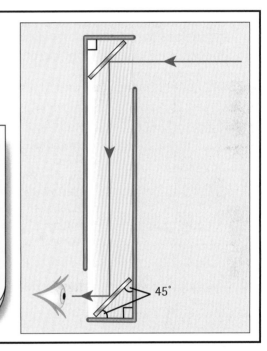

Comments

The diagram of the periscope that you draw must show the basic features clearly and in the correct position in relation to each other.

A simple periscope is a square tube with two plane mirrors set at 45° to the sides of the tube. By pointing the top of the tube towards the object being viewed, light enters and strikes the top mirror, is reflected down the tube onto the second mirror, and reflected into the eye of the observer.

Now try these!

Two cyclists are riding along a dark road at night. One is wearing black clothes and the other is wearing light-coloured clothes.

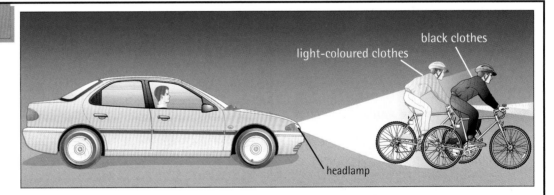

A car is driving behind the two cyclists. Light from the car headlamp shines on the cyclists.

1 What happens to the light when it reaches the light-coloured clothes? *(1 mark)*
2 On the drawing above, draw a ray of light to

show how light from the headlamp reaches the driver so that he can see the cyclist in the light-coloured clothes. Draw arrows to show the direction of the light. *(3 marks)*

3 What happens to the light when it reaches the black clothes? *(1 mark)*

Refraction

1 As light passes from one transparent material to another, its *speed changes* slightly.

- **Light slows down** as it passes from air into glass, water or perspex.

- **Light speeds up** as it passes out of those materials into the air.

- If the light passes into and out of one of these materials at right angles to the surface then the light ray passes through with no change of direction.

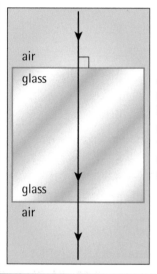

A ray of light striking a glass block at right angles passes through without changing direction

2 If the light passes into or out of a material at an angle then it will *change direction* as it crosses the boundary between the two materials.

- When the light is slowed down, its direction moves **towards the normal line**.

- When the light speeds up, its direction moves **away from the normal line**.

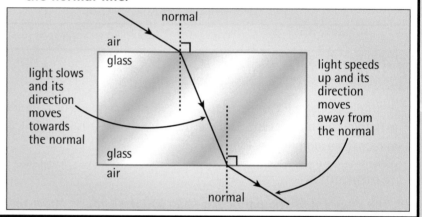

3 The process that causes light to *change direction* when it passes from one transparent material to another is called *refraction*.

- Often, refraction is responsible for distorting what we see.

- Light is refracted by different amounts as it passes through frosted glass so what we see is quite different to what is actually behind the glass.

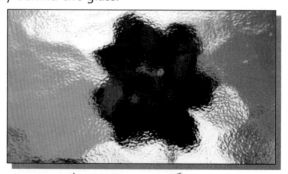

4 Refraction occurs as light passes through transparent blocks of different shapes.

- The change in direction of the light will depend on the angle at which it meets the surface of the block.

- Because of their shape, glass or perspex prisms refract light in particular ways.

prism

Remember

Refraction occurs when the speed of light changes as it passes from one transparent material to another.

Copy and complete

<u>Refraction</u>

Light _____ direction as it passes from one _____ material to another.

2 mins

1 What happens to the speed of light as it passes from air into water?

2 At what angle must a ray of light enter or leave another transparent material to ensure that it passes through without changing direction?

3 Why is what we see through frosted glass quite different to what is actually there?

Question and model answer

Explain the appearance of the pencil in this glass of water.

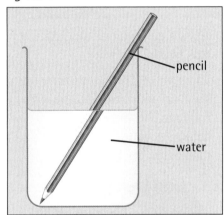

The pencil appears to be in a different position in the water. Light coming from the part of the pencil in the water is refracted as it leaves the container. Our eye perceives light to have travelled in a straight line from that part of the pencil so it appears to be in a different position to the part of the pencil above the water.

Comment

Make sure that you firstly state the appearance of the pencil in the glass of water. Then make sure that you give the reason for it looking that way. Remember that in this case light is coming from that part of the pencil in the water towards and into our eyes.

Now try this!

The diagram below shows the shapes and positions of five glass objects.

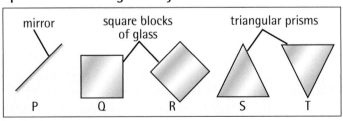

Harriet put a square of black card on top of each glass object and shone a ray of red light onto each object.

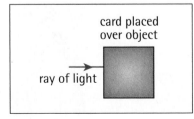

card placed over object

ray of light

The diagrams below show the rays of light going under the cards and coming out again. Which object is under each card? Write the correct letter below each diagram. One has been done for you. *(4 marks)*

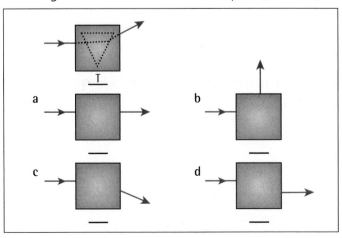

Colour

1 White light is a mixture of colours.

- If white light passes from air into a block of another transparent material, e.g. glass or perspex, the different colours of light are **refracted by different amounts**.

- This causes the white light to split into the colours of the spectrum. This process is called **dispersion**.

- The spectrum of white light contains **seven colours**.

- These can be remembered by using this short rhyme:

Richard	R	red
of	O	orange
York	Y	yellow
gave	G	green
battle	B	blue
in	I	indigo
vain	V	violet

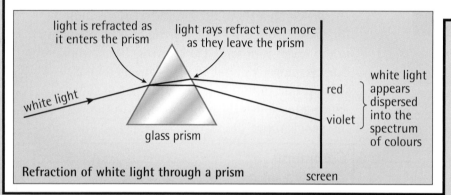

light is refracted as it enters the prism

light rays refract even more as they leave the prism

white light

red

violet

white light appears dispersed into the spectrum of colours

glass prism

screen

Refraction of white light through a prism

2 Different coloured lights can be added together.

- The primary colours of light are **red**, **green** and **blue**.

- These three primary colours of light can be added together to produce the three secondary colours – **yellow**, **cyan** and **magenta**.

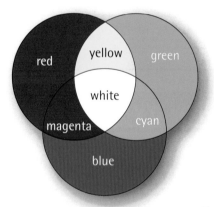

red   yellow   green

white

magenta   cyan

blue

3 Coloured filters are translucent – they only allow a specific colour of light to pass through them.

- In that way they **remove colours from white light**.
- A red filter will allow red light to pass through but it will absorb all of the other colours of the spectrum.
- The only colour of light that can be seen leaving a red filter is red.

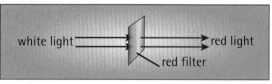

white light → → red light

red filter

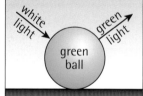

white light → green ball → green light

- Objects appear different when illuminated by different colours of light.

- When a green ball is illuminated with white light it reflects the green light and absorbs all of the other colours.

- When a green ball is illuminated by red light, there is no green light to reflect. The green ball will appear black because it absorbs the red light and doesn't reflect any light back to the observer.

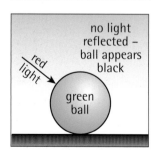

red light → green ball

no light reflected – ball appears black

The appearance of a green ball in white and red light

Remember

Red, orange, yellow, green, blue, indigo and violet are the seven colours in the spectrum of white light.

Copy and complete

Adding the primary colours of light

red + _____ ⟶ magenta

_____ + green ⟶ yellow

green + blue ⟶ _____

green + _____ + red ⟶ _____

Question and model answer

Natalie gets ready to go to a nightclub. She wears red lipstick, green earrings, a white dress and magenta coloured shoes.

Complete the table to show the appearance of each item under the different coloured lights in the nightclub.

	white light	blue light	yellow light	red light
red lipstick	red	**b**	**d**	red
green earrings	**a**	black	green	**e**
white dress	white	**c**	yellow	red
magenta shoes	magenta	blue	black	**f**

a green b black c blue d red e black f red

Comments

There is a lot of information here, which you need to understand before you work out your answers. Each of the four coloured objects is illuminated by four different colours of light in the nightclub. Start by looking for patterns in the table.

A coloured object appears that colour because it reflects that colour of light (a red object reflects red light); if that colour of light is shone onto the object then it will appear its actual colour.

White objects reflect all of the light shining onto them, so appear to be the colour of the light.

The red lipstick doesn't reflect blue light so it appears black. The magenta shoes reflect both red and blue light. If neither red nor blue light shines on them they will appear black.

Now try these!

Peter tried to obtain a mixture of red and green light. He used white light from a spotlight and slotted a red filter and a green filter in front of it as shown here:

The diagram below represents Peter's experiment.

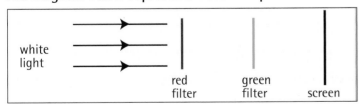

white light → red filter → green filter → screen

1a No light reached the screen. Explain why. *(2 marks)*

 b Peter cut a circular hole in the green filter. Describe what Peter would see on the screen. *(1 mark)*

2 Peter used two spotlights to shine a mixture of red and green light on to some red curtains.

 a What colour did the red curtains appear in this light? *(1 mark)*

 b Give the reasons why they appeared this colour. *(2 marks)*

Sound

1 Light and sound both travel from place to place as waves.

- Light travels at 300 000 000 metres per second, but sound travels much more slowly at about **330 metres per second through air.**

- Light can travel through a vacuum (through space) but sound cannot.

2 Waves have many similar features.

wave feature	definition
amplitude	The distance from the central position to the top/bottom of the wave.
frequency	The number of vibrations each second – measured in Hertz (Hz).
wavelength	The length of each complete wave – measured in metres (m).

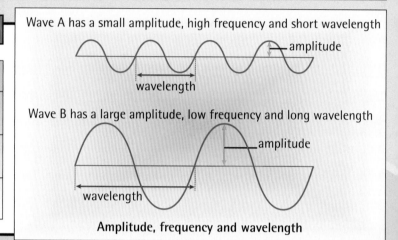

Wave A has a small amplitude, high frequency and short wavelength

Wave B has a large amplitude, low frequency and long wavelength

Amplitude, frequency and wavelength

3 The amplitude of a vibration affects the loudness of the sound that it produces.

- The **larger the amplitude** of the vibration the **louder** the sound produced.
- The **smaller the amplitude** of the vibration the **quieter** the sound produced.

4 The frequency of a vibration affects the pitch of the sound that it produces.

- The **greater the frequency** of vibration the **higher** is the pitch of the sound produced.
- The **lower the frequency** of vibration the **lower** is the pitch of the sound produced.

5 Sounds are heard when vibrations in the air cause the eardrum to vibrate.

- These vibrations are passed to the inner ear along three small bones called the **ossicles**.
- Humans can hear sounds that have frequencies from about **20 Hz** to about **20 000 Hz** but not everybody can hear across the entire range.
- Older people may not be able to hear the higher frequencies as well as younger people.
- Very loud sounds can cause damage to the eardrum. It can be stretched by the large amplitude of the vibration causing the sound, which can cause temporary pain and possibly long-term damage.
- Exposure to loud sounds for long periods can cause hearing loss because the excessive movement of the ossicles causes them to wear down more quickly.

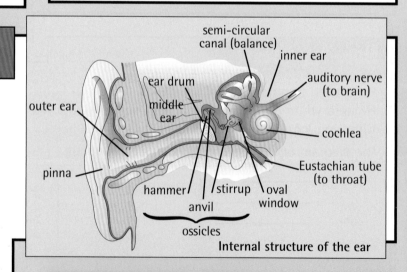

Internal structure of the ear

Remember

Exposure to loud sounds for long periods of time can result in deafness.

Copy and complete

	high	low
amplitude	loud sound	_____
frequency	_____ sound	low pitched sound

1 *What is the speed of sound in air?*
2 *What is the unit of frequency?*
3 *What part of the human ear can be damaged by very loud sounds?*

Question and model answer

A salvage ship uses echolocation to detect sunken ships. A high frequency sound wave is transmitted to the bottom of the sea. It is reflected from a wrecked ship 525 m below the surface. The echo of the sound is detected 0.7 seconds after it is transmitted.

How fast does sound travel in seawater?

$$\text{speed} = \frac{\text{distance travelled}}{\text{time taken}}$$

$$\frac{525 \times 2}{0.7} = 1500 \text{ m/s}$$

The speed of sound in seawater is 1500 m/s.

Comments

Always state the relationship you are going to use to calculate the answer.

In this case, the total distance travelled was 1050 m, 525 m from ship to wreck and 525 m back to the ship. It took the sound wave 0.7 seconds to cover that journey so the speed of the sound through the seawater was $\frac{525 \times 2}{0.7} = \frac{1050}{0.7} = 1500 \text{ m/s}$.

Always remember to show your working and to state the unit of the calculated answer.

Now try these!

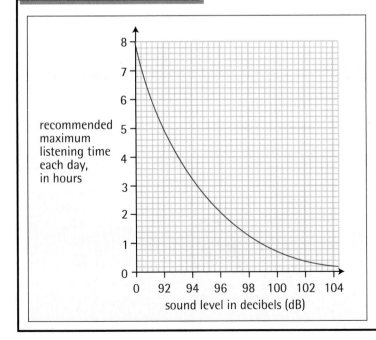

recommended maximum listening time each day, in hours

sound level in decibels (dB)

Sound levels are measured in decibels (dB). The graph shows the recommended maximum periods during which people should listen to sounds of different levels. For longer periods there could be serious damage to hearing.

1 What is the maximum time each day a person should listen to a personal stereo at 96 dB? *(1 mark)*

2 In what way could a sound of more than 120 dB damage the ear? *(1 mark)*

3 a Sally works for five hours in a nightclub. What should the maximum sound level be in the nightclub so that her hearing is not damaged? Use the graph to find your answer. *(1 mark)*

b How can ear plugs protect Sally's ears? *(1 mark)*

The solar system

1 The sun is the star at the centre of our solar system.

- A **star** is a massive luminous body which can have planets orbiting around it.

- **Planets** are bodies that orbit a sun. They are kept in orbit by the **gravitational attraction** that exists between them and the sun.

- Planets are sometimes visible in the night sky. This is because light from the sun is reflected from their surface towards us on Earth.

planet	av. distance to sun (millions of km)
Mercury	58
Venus	108
Earth	150
Mars	228
Jupiter	778
Saturn	1430
Uranus	2870
Neptune	4500
Pluto	5900

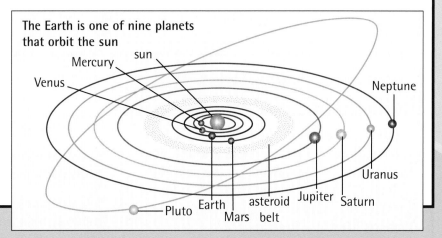

The Earth is one of nine planets that orbit the sun

2 As the Earth orbits the sun, it rotates on its axis.

- This rotation causes the **apparent daily movement** of the sun in the sky. The sun appears to **rise in the east** and move in an arc across the sky before **setting in the west**. Once the sun is below the western horizon we experience night-time.

- The Earth makes **one complete rotation** on its axis **each day**. This rotation is also the reason why the stars in the night sky appear to **rotate daily around the pole star**.

- The stars also seem to change position during the year because the Earth orbits the sun.

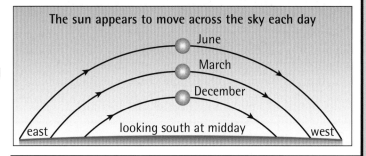

The sun appears to move across the sky each day

- These annual changes are responsible for the **different seasons** of the year.

- During **summer** in the Northern hemisphere, the **Earth is tilted towards the sun** so there are **more hours of daylight** than night-time.

- During **winter** in the Northern hemisphere the **Earth is tilted away from the sun** so there are **more hours of night-time** than daylight.

3 The apparent movement of the sun across the sky varies during the year.

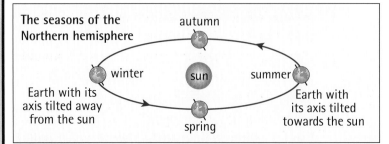

The seasons of the Northern hemisphere

- The sun rises higher in the sky in summer than it does in winter. This is because the **Earth's axis is tilted**.

Remember

The sun appears to move across the sky, due to the Earth's daily rotation and annual rotation around the sun.

Work-out!

Copy and complete

Position of planets in order from the sun

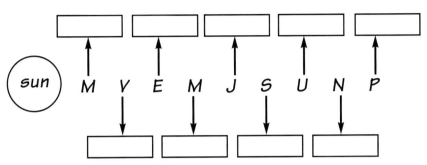

2 mins

1 How many planets are there in our solar system?
2 How many complete rotations on its axis does the Earth make each day?
3 Why do the stars seem to change position during the year?

Questions and model answers

Mars is the fourth planet from the sun. A day and night on Mars last a total of nearly 25 Earth hours and, like Earth, Mars has summers and winters during its year.

1 Explain why there is daytime and night-time on Mars.

Mars must rotate on its axis so that any one place on the planet's surface faces towards the sun for part of each rotation (daytime) and away from the sun for part of the rotation (night-time).

2 Explain what causes Mars to have seasons during its year.

Mars must rotate about a tilted axis. This means that for part of each year one hemisphere is tilted towards the sun and for the remaining part of the year it is tilted away from the sun.

Comments

Remember that an explanation requires you to give the reason for your answer.

If Mars did not rotate on its axis, one side of the planet would be in permanent darkness and the other half in permanent sunlight.

If Mars was not tilted on its axis then the climate at any one point on its surface would be constant throughout the year – it would not experience different seasons.

Now try these!

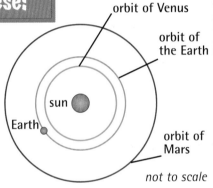

The diagram shows the orbits of the Earth, Mars and Venus. The position of the Earth is shown.

not to scale

A person on the Earth observes Mars and Venus.

1a On the diagram above, draw two more dots to show the position of Mars and Venus when they are closest to the Earth. Label the dot for Mars with a letter M and the dot for Venus with a letter V. *(1 mark)*

b Why is it easiest to see Mars when it is closest to the Earth? *(1 mark)*

2 What force keeps the Earth in its orbit and stops it flying off into space? *(1 mark)*

3 From the Earth, the moon always looks approximately the same size. What can you conclude from this about the orbit of the moon around the Earth? *(1 mark)*

4 The diagram shows the Earth in its orbit around the sun. What season is it in Britain? Explain your answer. *(2 marks)*

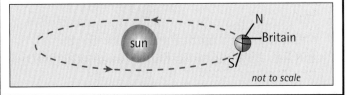

not to scale

Satellites

 1 A satellite is a body that orbits a planet.

- Some of the planets in the solar system have **natural satellites**. These are called **moons**.

- A moon is a natural object, which orbits a planet. The Earth has one natural satellite called **the Moon**.

- Just like all other objects in the night sky, the Moon and artificial satellites are visible because they **reflect light that comes from the sun**.

 2 Natural satellites (moons) orbit each planet in our solar system.

planet	number of natural satellites (moons)
Mercury	0
Venus	0
Earth	1
Mars	2
Jupiter	16
Saturn	18
Uranus	15
Neptune	8
Pluto	1

Jupiter and some of its moons

 3 The Earth also has many *artificial satellites*.

- These are pieces of machinery, which have many uses, launched into space.

- Some satellites collect **information about the weather**. These orbit close to the Earth so that they can make several orbits in a day to monitor changes in the weather.

- Some satellites are used for **communications** (telephone, radio and television), such as the one shown on the right.

- Some satellites can be used for **navigation** and for collecting a wide range of information from the Earth's surface.

- Other satellites, such as the **Hubble telescope**, have been put into orbit around the Earth to make observations of our solar system and the rest of the Universe.

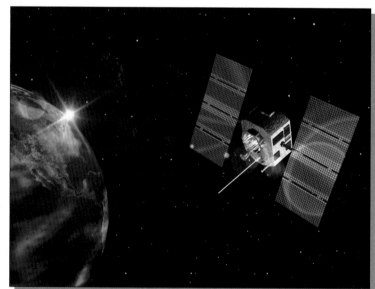

 4 Some of these artificial satellites are *geostationary*.

- At 36 000 km above the Earth these satellites orbit at exactly the same speed the Earth turns.

- They have an orbit time of 24 hours and remain directly above a particular point on the Earth's surface. They appear stationary to an observer on the Earth.

Remember

Artificial satellites are used to make observations of the Earth and explore the solar system.

Copy and complete

| collect information about the

w_____

s_____ | artificial satellites | collect information about the

E_____ |

| provide

c_____ |

1 What is another name for a natural satellite of a planet?

2 How many natural satellites orbit Jupiter?

3 How high does a geostationary satellite orbit above the Earth's surface?

Question and model answer

Why is it necessary for communications satellites to remain in the same position above the Earth's surface?

These satellites will need to be in continual contact with the transmitters and receivers, which form part of the communications network. As the communication signals travel in straight lines it is essential that the satellite is always in the sky above so that there are no breaks in the service.

Comments

The question tells you that communications satellites remain in the same position above the Earth's surface and asks you for reasons why. This must be related to what it is they are used for.

Orbiting several times a day is an advantage for satellites collecting information about the Earth and then transmitting it to a receiving station. Any satellite that is part of a communications network has to remain in a position where it is able to pass on the information at any time of the day or night.

Now try these!

Satellites can sometimes be seen in the night sky. They look like stars slowly moving across the sky.

1 We can see stars because they are light sources. They give out their own light. Satellites do not give out their own light. Explain why satellites can be seen in the clear night sky. *(2 marks)*

2 Sometimes a satellite suddenly stops being visible. However, you can usually see it again in another part of the sky later the same night. This can happen when there are no clouds in the sky and the satellite is overhead. Why does the satellite suddenly stop being visible? *(1 mark)*

3 Give **one** use of satellites in orbit around the Earth. *(1 mark)*

Energy sources

1 Everything that we do requires energy.

- We use vast quantities of energy to run our homes, industries and for transport.

- Burning fuels, such as **coal**, **oil** or **natural gas**, produces much of the energy that we use for these purposes. These are called **fossil fuels** because they were formed from dead plants and animals millions of years ago.

2 There are many other sources of energy.

- Some are these are **non-renewable**. These are energy resources that will eventually be used up because they were formed many millions of years ago and no more are being produced.

- The others are **renewable**. These are energy resources that are always being replaced.

energy resources		
non-renewable	renewable	
coal	biomass	hydroelectric
oil	wind	solar
natural gas	waves	tidal
nuclear		geothermal

3 The Sun is the ultimate source of most of the Earth's energy resources.

- With the exception of **tidal**, **geothermal** and **nuclear** energy, all of these energy resources obtained their energy from the sun or are constantly available because of energy from the sun.

- **Tidal energy** is created by the pull of the Moon on the seas as it moves around the Earth.

- **Geothermal energy** is from hot rocks deep inside the Earth's crust.

- **Nuclear energy** is produced from radioactive materials that are extracted from the Earth's crust.

4 Biomass is any plant or animal material that is used as a fuel or that is used to produce a fuel.

- **Wood** can be burned as a fuel. **Alcohol**, produced from sugar, can be used as a fuel for cars.

- Biomass is also the source of our food. We eat plants, or animals that have eaten plants.

5 Electricity provides a convenient way of using energy in our homes, offices and in industry.

- Electricity can be generated using all of the energy resources in the table (above).
- **Burning fossil fuels**, however, generates most of our electricity.
- Electricity has to be produced when it is needed because **it cannot be stored directly**. In order to store its energy, electricity can be used to produce a different energy resource in two ways.

  Electricity can be stored as **chemical energy** in the chemicals of batteries and transferred to electricity when needed.

  Electricity can be used to pump large quantities of water from a low reservoir up to a high reservoir behind a dam. The water is a store of **potential energy**. When the water is allowed to fall down the connecting pipe its energy of movement, **kinetic** energy, can be used to drive generators and be transferred back to electricity.

Remember

Renewable energy resources are always being replaced but non-renewable energy resources will eventually run out.

Work-out!

Copy and complete

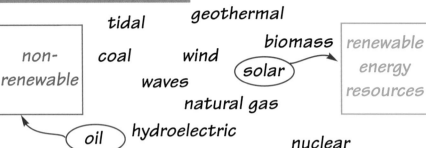

non-renewable

tidal

geothermal

coal wind biomass

waves solar → renewable energy resources

natural gas

oil hydroelectric

nuclear

2 mins

1 What is a renewable energy source?
2 What is biomass?
3 Why does electricity have to be produced when it is needed?

Question and model answer

Oil is an important energy resource. Describe how energy from the sun became stored in oil.

Millions of years ago plants used energy from the sun to grow. Animals would have eaten some of these plants. These living things died and as a result of chemical reactions deep underground oil was produced from their remains.

Comment

The process of formation of oil took many millions of years. Make sure that your answer includes reference to the fact that plants used energy from the sun to grow and that oil is formed from the remains of living things, both plants and animals.

Now try these!

1 The photographs show ways of getting energy from three different energy resources. On the line underneath each photograph, write the name of the energy resource. Choose from this list: **batteries biomass sunlight tides wind** *(3 marks)*

c _____

a _____   b _____

2 Name **one** fossil fuel. *(1 mark)*

3 Complete the sentence below.

The purpose of the machine in photograph **a** is to generate _____. *(1 mark)*

Conservation of energy

 1 Machines, both simple and complex, *transfer energy* from one type of energy to another.

In all energy transfers:

- the **total amount of energy before** and **after** the transfer is the **same**
- the **total amount of energy transferred** into the new form will always **be less** than in the original form
- some of the energy will be **dissipated** when the transfer takes place
- this energy will be 'lost' as **thermal energy** to the surroundings or be used to overcome friction in the workings of the machine
- if the amount of dissipated energy can be reduced to a minimum, then more of the original energy is available as a resource.
- the unit of energy is the **joule (J)**.

 2 The total amount of energy contained in an object is not a measure of the temperature of the object.

- The temperature is a measure of how hot an object is.
- A large, cool object, such as a bath full of water at 35 °C, stores much more thermal energy than a small, very hot object, such as a spark from a sparkler at 2000 °C.
- The spark is much hotter and the amount of energy needed to get it to that temperature may be much less than is needed to get the bath to its temperature.
- Although thermal energy is necessary to raise the temperature of an object, high temperatures do not always require large quantities of thermal energy.

 3 Thermal energy can be transferred from one place to another by particles in *three ways*.

- **Conduction:** energy is transferred from the **hotter part** of a substance to the **colder part**. The particles in the hot part are vibrating more because they have more energy. These vibrations are passed on to the cooler particles next to them, so the energy spreads through the material until all of the particles have the same energy.

- **Convection:** energy is transferred by the **movement of particles** within a liquid or gas. When a liquid or gas (fluid) becomes warm, it expands and becomes less dense. The less dense part of the fluid rises above the cooler part. The space it leaves behind is filled with cooler fluid. This can, in its turn, become warm and rise, as it becomes less dense.

- **Evaporation:** energy is transferred when the **particles near the surface of a liquid leave** the liquid to become a vapour. The escaping particles take some energy with them and leave the liquid slightly cooler.

 4 Thermal energy can also be transferred from one place to another directly by *radiation*.

- All objects **radiate** (give off) thermal energy.
- The hotter the object the more thermal energy it radiates.
- Thermal energy is radiated in the form of **infrared waves**.

Everything that happens involves a transfer of energy. The total amount of energy involved is conserved but some of it is wasted because it is 'lost' to the environment.

Copy and complete

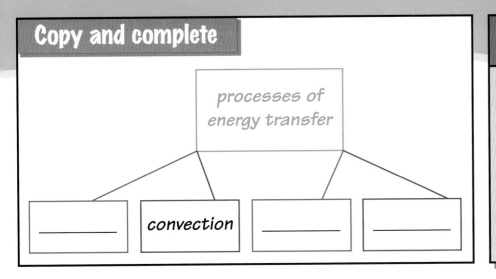

processes of
energy transfer

_____ | convection | _____ | _____

1 What is the unit of energy?
2 What is temperature a measure of?
3 Which process transfers thermal energy directly from one place to another?

Question and model answer

Non-metals, such as rubber, wool and cork, are poor conductors of thermal energy. They are described as good thermal insulators.

What can you say about the particles inside a good insulator?

The particles inside a good thermal insulator are likely to be either quite far apart or unable to vibrate very well.

Comments

The question tells you that a poor conductor of thermal energy is described as a good thermal insulator, so conduction and insulation are the opposite of each other. You must use what you know about the arrangements of particles inside these solids to explain how it prevents conduction from taking place.

Conduction occurs when particles vibrating because they have been warmed (have more energy) cause other particles near to them to vibrate. So the thermal energy moves through the substance.

If a substance is a good thermal insulator this process is prevented from taking place. This means that the particles are so far apart that the vibrating particles do not affect any others or the particles are arranged in such a way so that they are not able to vibrate.

Now try these!

1 In an iron rod the particles vibrate. If one end of the rod is heated, the vibrating particles transfer energy to neighbouring particles, which are not vibrating so violently. Name this process. *(1 mark)*

2 An electric immersion heater is put at the bottom of a large tank of water. The water next to the heater becomes warm.

   a What happens to the warmed water next to the heater? Give a reason for your answer. *(2 marks)*

   b Why can thermal energy not be transferred in this way in an iron rod? *(1 mark)*

3 In a liquid, some of the particles have enough kinetic energy to escape from the surface. This process happens even when the liquid is well below its boiling point.

   a What is the process called? *(1 mark)*

   b How will this affect the temperature of the liquid left in the container? *(1 mark)*

Answers

Biology

Life processes

2 mins

1　Eye, ear, nose, tongue and skin

2　Plants: leaf, root, flower, ovary
   Animals: kidney, eye, muscle, ovary, brain

3　Motor car is not a living thing because it does not reproduce or grow.

Now try these!

1　a Every month/four weeks/28 days.
   b Oviduct or fallopian tube.

2　Fetus, nine.

Cells

2 mins

1　The cell membrane controls what passes into and out of the cell.

2　Chemical reactions take place in the cytoplasm.

3　The green pigment is called chlorophyll.

4　The cell wall provides support for plant cells, helping them to keep their shape.

Now try these!

1

part	letter of part
cell wall	e
cytoplasm	a
nucleus	b
vacuole	d

2　Any two from a, b, and f.

Food and digestion

2 mins

1　Fibre helps the passage of food through the body.

2　Meat, fish and cheese contain protein.

3　Energy and chemicals are the two most important things provided by our food.

4　Enzymes increase the speed at which the chemical reactions of digestion take place.

Now try these

1a One may be more active.

1b Carbohydrates and fats.

2a 300 mg

2b The boy's bones/teeth are still growing.

The skeleton and movement

2 mins

1　The heart and lungs are protected by the rib cage.

2　Ligaments hold bones together at joints.

3　Tendons are strong, non-stretchy tissues.

Now try these!

1a

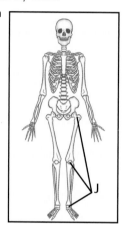

1b So that we can bend/move/walk.

2a Ribs

2b Lower jaw

2c Calcium

3a Muscles

3b Upwards

Respiration

2 mins

1　Alveoli (air sacs) are at the end of bronchioles.

2　Oxygen is needed for aerobic respiration to take place.

3　Respiration (the reaction between glucose and oxygen) takes place in the cells of the body.

Now try these!

1a P

1b S

2a Oxygen

2b Carbon dioxide

3　So that oxygen/carbon dioxide/gases can pass through the walls quickly/easily.

4　Any one from:
   • so that a lot of oxygen can be absorbed/taken in
   • the body needs a lot of oxygen
   • so that a lot of carbon dioxide can be removed.

Human reproduction

2 mins

1　The testes produce sperm.

2　The ovaries release the ova.

3　The usual length of the menstrual cycle is 28 days.

Now try these!

1a It cushions/protects the baby.

1b Placenta

1c Alcohol

2　Muscles contract/contractions.

Staying healthy

2 mins

1　Pathogens are organisms that cause disease.

2　Any two from: cholera, typhoid, tuberculosis and syphilis.

3　Any two from: influenza, polio, German measles and AIDS.

4　Antibiotics attack bacteria that cause disease.

Now try these!

1　It took one day for the amount of bacteria to get to a significant level, making them ill.

2　The antibiotics/medicine killed all of the bacteria.

Photosynthesis

2 mins

1　Chlorophyll captures light for photosynthesis.

2　Chloroplasts contain the green pigment.

3　Most of the oxygen produced during photosynthesis is released into the atmosphere and used by other living things.

Now try these!

1　Glucose

2a To absorb enough/more light.

2b Chloroplasts, containing chlorophyll.

Plant growth

2 mins

1　Nitrogen, potassium and phosphorous are needed by plants for healthy growth.

2　Fertilisers are often added to the soil.

3　Root hair cells absorb water and dissolved salts from the soil.

Now try this!

   Oxygen is produced during photosynthesis and used up in respiration. Carbon dioxide is used up during photosynthesis and is produced during respiration.

Variation

2 mins

1 A group of living things, with many similar features, that can successfully interbreed.
2 Eye/hair colour, nose shape and ear shape.
3 Quality of diet and amount of exercise are two factors that will affect how tall a child grows.

Now try this!

1a They have inherited different characteristics/different genes.
1b Any two from:
- amount of food
- type of food
- amount of water
- level of disease/quality of health
- level of stress
- temperature/climate
- exercise/amount of space.

Classification

2 mins

1 Five
2 Conifers and flowering plants.
3 Invertebrates are animals that do not have a backbone.

Now try these!

1 a: insects   b: amphibians
   c: molluscs   d: reptiles
2 a and c

Inheritance

2 mins

1 In pairs.
2 One that does not show itself (unless there are two recessive versions present) because it is overpowered by a dominant gene.
3 Deoxyribonucleic acid.

Now try these!

1 Selective breeding
2 Any one from:
- resistance to disease
- fast growth rate
- high fertility
- long life
- good skin for making leather
- docile temperament
- hardiness/resistance to weather.

Habitats

2 mins

1 The place where a plant or animal normally lives.
2 Food, water and space.
3 Competition between them.

Now try this!

Any two from:
- they live in/close to their food
- they are not washed away
- protection/they cannot be seen.

Food webs

2 mins

1 The number of other species, called predators, which eat it for food.
2 The size of the population.
3 Because the concentrations of poisons inside them are relatively low.

Now try these!

1 Any one from:
   Herring:
- there are fewer eggs
- fewer herring eggs hatch
- herring eggs are removed.
   Cod have fewer herring to eat/less food.
2 The habitat of sandeels is reduced/destroyed/removed. Puffins have fewer sandeels to eat.

Chemistry

States of matter

2 mins

1 $-38\,°C$
2 Liquids and gases.
3 In a fixed, regular pattern.

Now try these!

1 $121\,°C$
2a Q
2b S

Changes of state

2 mins

1 Change the temperature of a substance.
2 Freezing (solidification)
3 It changes from a gas to a liquid.

Now try these!

1

element	m.p.	b.p.	physical state
bromine	-7	59	liquid
chlorine	-101	-34	gas
fluorine	-220	-188	gas
iodine	114	184	solid

2 Gas
3a Gas   3b Liquid   3c Solid

Atoms and molecules

2 mins

1 Protons and neutrons
2 Atomic number
3 A molecule is a combination of the same or different atoms.

Now try these!

1a R and Z   1b L
2 16
3 11

Elements, compounds and mixtures

2 mins

1 One
2 Cu
3 Four

Now try these!

1 C
2 D
3 A and B
4 A and D
5 C

The periodic table

2 mins

1 Pb
2 Tungsten
3 Tin

Now try these!

1 Hydrogen
2a Region 3
2b Region 1
2c Region 2
3 Any one from:
- it is a compound
- it is not an element
- it is made up of more than one element.

Answers

Separating mixtures

2 mins

1. Filtration
2. Solids from liquids or mixtures of liquids.
3. Evaporation, distillation and fractional distillation.

Now try these!

1a. E102 and E160
1b. Another spot drawn above the spot for drink Y and at the same height as E102.
1c. Count the number of spots above the spot of drink.
2a. Filter paper absorbs water.
2b. It might dissolve/smudge/run/separate out.

Physical changes

2 mins

1. Solubility is calculated by finding the maximum mass of a substance that can be dissolved in 100 g of water at a particular temperature.
2. Solute
3. A solution into which no more solute will dissolve.

Now try these!

1a. solution   1b. insoluble   1c. solvent
2. Any one from: filter it/filtration, pour off the liquid, centrifuge it.
3. It evaporated/became a gas/vapour.

Geological changes

2 mins

1. The breaking up of rocks
2. Sedimentary rock
3. For example, marble and slate

Now try these!

example	weathering	erosion	neither
The stones in an old wall have been pushed apart by the roots of weeds.	✓		
An old granite gravestone is still smooth and shiny.			✓
A clay flower pot in the garden has crumbled and broken into pieces during the winter.	✓		
Some soil has been washed from a flower bed by rain.		✓	

2. Freezing/freeze-thaw/acid rain/ chemical weathering

Chemical reactions

2 mins

1. Reduction reactions
2. Rusting
3. Sulphur dioxide

Now try these!

1a. A and D
1b. C
2. Any two from:
   - paint them
   - grease them
   - oil them
   - galvanise them
   - plate/chrome/coat them
   - coat/cover them in plastic.

Word equations

2 mins

1. Reactants
2. Products
3. It is exactly the same.

Now try these!

1a. Blue
1b. Black
2. copper oxide + sulphuric acid $\longrightarrow$ copper sulphate + water
3. To separate/remove the copper oxide.

Metals and non-metals

2 mins

1. Magnesium, copper and chlorine
2. Mercury
3. Metal salts and hydrogen

Now try these!

1a. Any one from:
   - gold
   - iron
   - magnesium.
1b. Sulphur or phosphorus
1c. Iron
1d. Iron sulphide
2. Magnesium sulphide

The reactivity series

2 mins

1. A reaction when a more reactive metal reacts with a compound of a less reactive metal.
2. Calcium
3. A list of metals in order of reactivity – from the most to the least reactive.

Now try these!

1a. copper + silver nitrate $\longrightarrow$ copper nitrate + silver
1b. Copper
    Silver
    Platinum
2. Iron, because it is more reactive.

Acids and alkalis

2 mins

1. Hydrogen
2. Blue
3. Metal salts and water.

Now try these!

1.

	acidic or alkaline	colour of U.I. paper
bee sting (pH2)	acidic	red
wasp sting (pH10)	alkaline	blue/purple

2a. Any one from:
   - bicarbonate toothpaste
   - washing soda.
2b. Any one from:
   - vinegar
   - lemon juice.

Neutralisation

2 mins

1. Water
2. Lime
3. Sulphur dioxide and nitrogen dioxide.

Now try these!

1a. Alkaline
1b. Forms a solution with a pH of about 8.5; it is not poisonous.
2. Sodium hydrogencarbonate + nitric acid $\longrightarrow$ carbon dioxide + water + sodium nitrate
3. Carbon dioxide

Physics

Electrical charge

2 mins

1   Repel each other.
2   They flow away from the point they are produced.
3   Amperes (A)

Now try these!

1   By rubbing it/by friction.
2   Negatively-charged because B is attracted - unlike charges attract.
3   Towards A/to the left.

Electrical circuits

2 mins

1   It is the same.
2   Current splits and rejoins.
3   More than one.

Now try these!

1   pick-up wire, metal wheel
2   Any one from:
    • it completes the circuit
    • it acts as a switch.
3   Any one from:
    • he does not complete the circuit
    • he does not connect the floor to the wire mesh ceiling.

Electromagnets

2 mins

1   Magnetic field
2   It concentrates the magnetic field.
3   A switch that uses an electromagnet.

Now try these!

1a
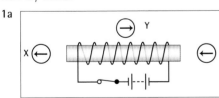

1b
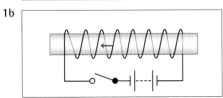

1c   North
2   Reverse the battery or wind the coil in the opposite direction.
3a   Poles are N-S-N-S
3b   They attract each other.

Speed

2 mins

1   The rate at which something is moving.
2   Distance travelled and time taken.
3   Metres per second (m/s).

Now try these!

1a $260 \div 180 = 1.44$ m/min
1b $1.44 \div 60 = 0.024$ m/s
2a $260 \div 1.08 = 240.7$ s
2b   Any one from:
     • it takes time to reach this speed
     • it slows down before the end
     • it is not the average speed.

Unbalanced forces

2 mins

1   No effect.
2   The force produced when two substances that are touching move past each other; the force that resists the motion of objects.
3   Air resistance.

Now try these!

1   They are equal/balanced.
2a   The force of weight is greater than friction.
2bi It increases.
2bii It decreases.
2c   It increases/it gets faster.

Turning forces

2 mins

1   Pivot
2   Either increase the size of the force or move the point of application further away from the pivot.
3   Balanced

Now try these!

1   $5000 \times 8 = 40\,000$ Nm
2   4 m
3   3750 N

Pressure

2 mins

1   Force and area.
2   Newton per square metre (N/m^2).
3   Reduce our pressure by spreading our weight over a larger area.

Now try these!

1   $175 \div 7 = 25$ N/cm^2
2   Any one from:
    • greater than 27 N/cm^2
    • greater than the pressure in the tyre.
3   $95 \times 30 = 2850$ N

Reflection

2 mins

1   300 000 000 m/s
2   Luminous objects produce their own light.
3   A normal line.

Now try these!

1   It is reflected.

2
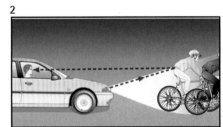

3   It is absorbed.

Refraction

2 mins

1   It slows down.
2   At right angles to the surface.
3   Because light is refracted by different amounts by frosted glass.

Now try this!

a   Q
b   P
c   S
d   R

Answers

Colour

2 mins

1 Seven
2 Violet
3 Blue

Now try these!

1a Only red light passes through the red filter. The red light is absorbed/stopped by the green filter.
1b A circle of red light.
2a Red
2b The green light is absorbed; the red light is scattered/reflected.

Sound

2 mins

1 330 m/s
2 Hertz (Hz)
3 Ear drum

Now try these!

1 Two hours
2 It would damage the eardrum/cochlea/middle ear make you deaf/tinnitus/ringing in the ear.
3a 92 dB
3b Any one from:
- they make the sound quieter
- they absorb the sound
- they prevent damage to the eardrum
- they stop the sound.

The solar system

2 mins

1 Nine
2 One
3 Because the Earth orbits the sun.

Now try these!

1a

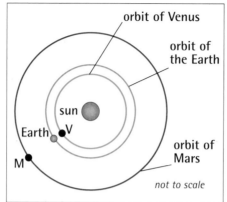

not to scale

1b Any one from:
- it is brightest
- it looks bigger/biggest
- you can see it at night.

2 Gravity
3 It is circular or it is always the same distance from the Earth.
4 Winter. Any one reason from:
- the northern hemisphere is tilted away from the Sun
- Britain is in the part of the Earth which is tilted away from the Sun
- the Sun's rays hit the Earth at more of an angle
- the Sun appears lower in the sky
- night is longer than day.

Satellites

2 mins

1 A moon
2 16
3 36 000 km

Now try these!

1 They reflect/scatter light from the sun.
2 It goes into the shadow of the Earth.
3 Any one from:
- weather forecasting
- navigation/position finding
- communications
- astronomy/looking at the stars
- to take pictures of the Earth
- defence/spying
- TV/telephone/radio.

Energy sources

2 mins

1 Energy sources that are always being replaced.
2 Any plant or animal material that is used as a fuel or to produce fuel .
3 It cannot be stored directly.

Now try these!

1a Wind
1b Sunlight
1c Tides
2 Any one from:
- coal
- gas/methane
- oil/petrol
- peat.
3 Electricity

Conservation of energy

2 mins

1 Joule (J)
2 How hot something is.
3 Radiation

Now try these!

1 Conduction
2a It will rise. Any one reason from:
- it expands
- it becomes less dense
- the particles are further apart
2b Any one from:
- the atoms/particles in a solid cannot move around
- the atoms/particles are bonded tightly
- iron is not a fluid
- atoms cannot move around
- iron has a fixed shape
3a Evaporation
3b Any one from:
- it will get colder
- it will decrease
- it will lose thermal energy.